Becoming Good, Becoming Holy

On the Relationship of Christian Ethics and Spirituality

Mark O'Keefe, O.S.B.

PAULIST PRESS
New York/Mahwah, N.J.

Several of the chapters in the book have appeared in earlier form in various journals:

Chapter 1: "Catholic Moral Theology and Christian Spirituality," *New Theology Review* 7 (May 1994): 60–73.

Chapter 3: "Fundamental Option and the Three Ways," *Studies in Formative Spirituality* 13 (February 1992): 73–83.

Chapter 4: "*Theosis* and the Christian Life," *Église et Théologie* 25 (January 1994): 47–63.

Chapter 6: "Authentic Relationships: Justice, Love, and Christian Spirituality," *New Blackfriars* 76 (January 1995): 30–43.

Chapter 7: "Christian Prayer and Moral Decision Making," *Spiritual Life* 40 (Fall 1994): 169–78.

Chapter 8: "Discernment and Christian Moral Decision Making," *Journal of Spiritual Formation* 15 (February 1994): 65–83.

Library of Congress Cataloging-in-Publication Data

O'Keefe, Mark, 1956-
    Becoming good, becoming holy : on the relationship of Christian ethics and spirituality / Mark O'Keefe.
        p. cm.
    Includes bibliographical references.
    ISBN 0-8091-3593-0 (alk. paper)
    1. Christian ethics—Catholic authors. 2. Spirituality—Catholic Church 3. Catholic Church—Doctrines. I. Title.
BJ1249.037 1995   95-16977
241'.042—dc20   CIP

Published by Paulist Press
997 Macarthur Boulevard
Mahwah, NJ 07430

Printed and bound in the
United States of America

CONTENTS

iv   *Contents*

Christian Life Focused in Decisions

ACKNOWLEDGMENTS

I would like to express my gratitude to the many people who have assisted me in the preparation of this book. Dick Sparks, a friend, fellow moral theologian, and editor at Paulist Press, offered the encouragement that resulted both in my earlier book for the Paulist Press *What Are They Saying About* series, and in drawing together my thoughts for this present work. I thank him and Paulist Press for their help and encouragement.

I was able to complete this work while on a semester sabbatical. For that opportunity, I am grateful to Archabbot Timothy Sweeney, O.S.B., Eugene Hensell, O.S.B., Harry Hagan, O.S.B., Tom Walters, and my faculty colleagues at St. Meinrad School of Theology. During the sabbatical, I lived alone in the quiet solitude of the rectory of Holy Cross parish in Saint Croix, Indiana. I am grateful to Richard Hindel, O.S.B. and to his successor as parish administrator, Alan McIntosh, O.S.B., and to the people of the parish for the wonderful balance of hospitality and "space."

Many colleagues and friends have read parts of this work over the years of its development and I am grateful for their comments and suggestions. I would like to acknowledge their invaluable assistance: Aurelius Boberek, O.S.B., Mark Ciganovich, O.Carm., Godfrey Mullen, O.S.B., Matthias Newman, O.S.B., Jerry Neufelder, Morris Pelzel, and Kurt Stasiak, O.S.B. I offer a special word of thanks to Greg Luyet who served as my research assistant during my sabbatical.

I am grateful to the students and alumni of St. Meinrad School of Theology whose questions have challenged me and whose generous dedication to God's service in contemporary society has inspired me in countless ways.

INTRODUCTION

Some thirty years ago, the Second Vatican Council offered a challenging direction for the renewal of Roman Catholic moral theology:

> Special care should be given to the perfecting of moral theology. Its scientific presentation should draw more fully on the teaching of Holy Scripture and should throw light upon the exalted vocation of the faithful in Christ and their obligation to bring forth fruit in charity for the life of the world.[1]

Shortly after the council, moral theologian Josef Fuchs suggested that this conciliar text directed Catholic moral theology to present the Christian moral life as Christocentric, focused on vocation rather than on law, responsive in character, directed distinctively to Christian men and women, and clearly indicating the "exalted nature" of the Christian calling.[2]

It is certain that the council challenged moral theology to look beyond an exclusive focus on moral problems and acts, norms and decision-making. The task of moral theology, after all, involves shedding light on the "exalted vocation" of Christians in the world. Pope John Paul II's recent encyclical, *Veritatis splendor*, offers emphatic confirmation of this more "exalted" conciliar view of moral theology as directed ultimately to the source of all good, to communion with God.[3] In fact, the conciliar and papal challenge to Catholic moral theology suggests

1

a close relationship between the tasks of moral theology and spirituality.[4] In short, the Christian effort to become truly good is implicitly aimed at becoming truly holy.

At the same time that it was summoning moral theology to renewal, the council reminded Christians that all of the baptized are called to holiness.[5] Sanctity can no longer be understood as the privileged domain of a spiritual elite such as clergy and religious. But the path to holiness, as the Christian spiritual tradition has always maintained, is inescapably both moral and spiritual. Growth in holiness requires overcoming sin, building up virtue, and growing in charity. The council's "universal call to holiness," then, is implicitly but necessarily a call to Christian moral living. In short, the Christian effort to become truly holy requires the effort to become truly good.

In this book, I set out to study the relationship between moral theology and spirituality. As a moral theologian, I believe that the clear establishment of the link between the two disciplines is essential to the continued authentic renewal of Catholic moral theology. Failure to establish this link prevents moral theology from offering truly adequate assistance to men and women seeking to be faithful to their vocation in Christ.

Further, I presume that it is one of the purposes of Christian spirituality to guide Christians to the holiness that is virtually their baptismal birthright. If this is so, it is essential to Christian spirituality that the link with moral theology be clearly established, since moral growth is essential on the path to holiness.

Very few contemporary moral theologians would deny a close relationship between Christian ethics and spirituality. Virtually every recent introduction to Christian ethics alludes to this relationship. At the same time, however, very few of the introductions provide any sustained discussion of the link with spirituality. This is, of course, not necessarily a criticism since these works seek to introduce the reader to the rather broad range of contemporary moral theology. Perhaps more surprising is the relative absence of book–length examinations of ethics and spirituality, and of a larger body of literature on their relationship. The historical survey in chapter 1 will suggest some reasons for this relative neglect of the topic of ethics and spirituality.

I have undertaken this study in order to offer some suggestions to fill what seems to me to be a major lacuna in the contemporary academic disciplines of Christian ethics and spirituality. My personal interest in this topic probably dates from the time of my dissertation work on the thought of Bernard Häring. Reading his vast body of work, one is unavoidably struck by Häring's concern to relate moral theology to the "exalted vocation" of Christian people, and more specifically to relate ethics and spirituality. Certainly my own subsequent teaching of, and academic reflection on, the Christian moral life has only served to further my interest. Perhaps this interest has also been heightened by the fact that I teach people preparing for professional ministry, ordained and lay, who often challenge me to show the relevance of the concerns of academic moral theology for the lived experience of ordinary Christians. Sharing the faith journey with many students through spiritual direction also reveals the important connection between their moral and spiritual striving, as I find true in my own life journey. I find, too, that the Benedictine spirituality in which I have personally been formed—contrary to the opinion of those today who maintain that monastic spirituality is inherently world-denying or even dualistic—presupposes an intimate link between morality and spirituality in the daily events and encounters of the monastic life.

An Overview

This book offers a number of different perspectives on the relationship of ethics and spirituality in the Christian life. Rather than a systematic and comprehensive study, it examines different areas or facets of the interrelationship between moral theology and spirituality. Each chapter can be read on its own, independent of the others and in whatever order the reader wishes. But, at the same time, there is a development in the topics covered in successive chapters that is meant to suggest a broader perspective on the relationship of the moral and spiritual life.

Chapter 1 establishes the foundation for subsequent topics by surveying the history of the relationship of moral theology and spirituality. It briefly summarizes contemporary trends in both disciplines that aid or inhibit the establishment of a closer connection between them. Finally, it offers some suggestions for the continued development of both disciplines.

The next three chapters develop the notion that there is an essential dynamism to the Christian life, a dynamism that is essentially both moral and spiritual. Chapter 2 focuses on the experience of Christian conversion as the foundation for the moral and spiritual lives of Christians and therefore as the foundation of the disciplines that study them. Conversion is never, however, an entirely accomplished fact; and so, the experience of conversion directs the Christian to a life of continual conversion. Chapter 3, in a sense, picks up at that point by examining two approaches for explaining the shape of ongoing Christian conversion. One is the traditional "Three Ways" of purgation, illumination, and union; the other is the more contemporary discussion of fundamental option; and it is suggested that each approach enriches the other. Chapter 2, therefore, focuses on the "starting point" of the Christian path, while chapter 3 examines the dynamic integration that the path requires. Chapter 4 focuses on the goal of the Christian way in Eastern Orthodox terms as *theosis* (deification), that is, as participation in the divine nature. But while *theosis* is a future goal, it is also a present reality that makes present demands on the life of the Christian. These three chapters, then, look at the dynamism of ongoing conversion in the Christian life and highlight the essential relationship of moral and spiritual striving throughout the Christian life.

Chapters 5 and 6 broaden the focus from the life of individual Christians to the human relationships that are essential to authentic human living. Both contemporary moral theology and spirituality have come to see that they must take a relational, social perspective on the Christian life. An examination of the relationship of these disciplines, therefore, also requires taking this perspective. Chapter 5 examines the interconnection of spirituality, justice, and love. It suggests that the Christian life requires the search for authentic relationships as the necessary foundation for the full mutuality of trinitarian life to which men and women have been invited to participate in Christ. "Right relationships" (justice) are essential to the fully mutual relationships (love) that are the goal of both the Christian moral life and the Christian spiritual life. Chapter 6 continues the discussion of authentic relationships by examining the relationship of liturgy and the moral life. The liturgy celebrates the authentic relationships with God and with other persons that Christ has made possible through his victory over sin. At the same time, the liturgy forms Christians for the life of discipleship and for the authentic relationships that characterize the manifestation of God's reign.

Chapters 7 and 8 move to the more concrete ramifications of the relationship of ethics and spirituality by focusing on moral decision-making. Chapter 7 examines one aspect of the relationship between prayer and moral decision-making by focusing on how prayer forms the Christian as a moral agent, that is, as a person who makes decisions. Chapter 8 looks more closely at decision-making itself, suggesting that the moral decisions of Christians must be understood as the discernment of God's will through attention to a variety of sources for discovering the divine will in concrete situations.

The book concludes with a constructive summary statement that draws the various chapters together into a broader account of the relationship of ethics and spirituality.

Some Final Caveats

I write on the relationship of moral theology and spirituality as a moral theologian, interested in but without specific expertise in the contemporary discipline of spirituality. My perspective is therefore necessarily limited. At the same time, my purpose is not to offer the definitive word on the relationship of moral theology and spirituality nor even on any of the individual topics treated. In the absence of a large body of significant literature on the relationship of ethics and spirituality by experts in either field, I offer this work as suggestive and as a basis for further discussion. Similarly, I do not propose that this book is an adequate introduction to either Christian ethics or to Christian spirituality. At the same time, I believe that reflection on the kinds of topics treated in this book is essential to an adequate introduction to either discipline.

It is probably already quite obvious to the reader that I write as a *Roman Catholic* moral theologian. In chapter 4, I enter into explicit dialogue with the Orthodox theological tradition in its concept of *theosis*. Although I do not offer other chapters that focus explicitly on dialogue with other Christian traditions, I believe that contemporary Christian ethics has become sufficiently ecumenical that the influence of and dialogue with ethicists outside the Roman Catholic tradition will be apparent. At some points, my perspectives and emphases will be distinctively Catholic, but I hope that colleagues from other Christian traditions will find even these sections to be fruitful for reflection—even if only by way of some disagreement with my emphases.

A final caveat concerns all of the language of "striving," "effort," and "task" that runs throughout the book. A faculty colleague, on reading a section of the book, remarked that all of this "effort language" smacked of at least semi–Pelagianism. This friendly remark gave me pause. Perhaps monks have a particular tendency to Pelagianism (Pelagius was a monk!) since there is so much of the language of "striving" in the monastic search for God. Perhaps moral theologians share a similar tendency because they do focus so much attention on human agency, freedom, and choice. Ultimately, of course, God is the source of all good action and of all moral and spiritual growth; and in recognizing a certain tension between God's initiative and human cooperation, between grace and human freedom, we must not lose sight of the priority of God's action. Still, all of that cautioning notwithstanding, there is no denying that there is quite simply a lot of effort, discipline, and striving involved in both moral and spiritual growth, in becoming both good and holy.

Setting the Stage

1

ETHICS AND SPIRITUALITY: PAST, PRESENT, FUTURE

Although we commonly distinguish between a Christian moral life and a Christian spiritual life, in the daily existence of Christian men and women these "lives" are, of course, one. There is no "moral life" separate from a "spiritual life." In the actual living of the Christian life, efforts to avoid sin, to grow in prayer, to make good moral decisions, and to grow in virtue are intimately intertwined. As lived experience shows and as the collective moral and spiritual wisdom of the Christian community has made clear, there can be no stable victory over serious sin in our lives without the assistance of grace encountered in prayer, both private and communal. Similarly, there can be no sustained growth in a habit and disposition of prayer without the overcoming of serious sin and a growth in good moral living.

Because of the interconnectedness of moral and spiritual striving in the daily experience of the Christian life, one might expect that the disciplines of Catholic moral theology and of Christian spirituality would also be closely interrelated. One might expect that, in their efforts to aid the growth of an authentic Christian existence, the two disciplines would be marked by mutual interchange. Such is not the case—at least not in a sustained and systematic way.

It is clear that moral theology and spirituality are distinct and separate disciplines with distinct objects of study and methodologies. There is no reason to suggest an attempt to return

the patristic period—and thus its spirituality—was utterly Christocentric. Christ was understood to be "the measure, the model, and the goal of the spiritual life."[3] The whole of the believer's life was made possible by salvation in Christ, nurtured and rooted in the liturgy, and aimed at conformity and union with Christ. In this Christocentric perspective—in line with the synoptic emphasis on discipleship and the Pauline focus on "being in Christ"—there could be no separation between one's moral striving and one's life of prayer and worship.

From the patristic period comes the effort to identify and analyze stages or levels in the Christian life. Although various patristic and medieval theologians identified diverse numbers of stages—from two stages (Evagrius' distinction between the practical life and *gnosis*) to thirty such stages (St. John Climacus' degrees)—gradually the identification of these stages came to be identified as the Three Ways. The Ways could be identified as beginner, proficient and perfect (following Origen and Evagrius Ponticus) or as purgative, illuminative, and unitive (following Pseudo-Dionysius). By the late medieval period these two sets of terms became virtually interchangeable. In any case, however many stages were identified or whatever names were given to them, two common elements appear in each of the designations: a sense of growth or progression in the Christian life and an essential connection between spiritual and moral growth in every authentic Christian life.

In St. Thomas' *Summa Theologiae*, we see the unity of the theological enterprise at its height, before its division into the specializations of dogmatic and moral theology (the latter including spiritual theology within its scope). What we today call moral theology and spirituality were elements of the wider theological synthesis exemplified by St. Thomas' *Summa*. The Christian life, moral and spiritual, was understood in the total context of the person's striving to attain the ultimate end, the beatific vision. In this synthesis, the moral life could no more be separated from striving for union with God than moral theology could be separated from its wider theological roots.

St. Thomas continues the threefold division of the Christian life into beginners, proficients, and the perfect with its inherent connection between morality and spirituality (*ST* IIa-IIae, q.24, a.9; q.183, a.4). But the subtleties of the interrelation of moral and spiritual striving are further evident in the discussion of the virtues, acquired and infused, in which charity directed ultimately toward God becomes the "form" of the virtues (*ST* IIa-IIae, q.23, a.8). In this Thomistic context, the Christian moral life is the life of virtue formed by love and empowered and transformed by grace.

The development of moral theology as a separate discipline distinct from dogmatic theology began in the sixteenth and seventeenth centuries with the development of extended commentaries on the *Secunda pars* of the *Summa Theologiae*, such as those of Thomas de Vio (d. 1534), Francis de Vitoria (d. 1546), and Francis Suarez (d. 1617). The Counter-Reformation period also saw the emergence of a new genre of manuals or textbooks of moral theology—the *Institutiones theologiae moralis*.[4] Some of the earliest of these manuals were those of the Spanish Jesuits, most notably, John Azor (d. 1603). At about the same time, we see the appearance of great classics of spirituality in the writings of St. Ignatius, St. Teresa of Avila, and St. John of the Cross—spiritual classics which do not stem from classical speculative theology.[5]

The moral theology of the sixteenth and seventeenth centuries, however, manifested not merely a process of developing theological specialization but a bifurcation in the inherent relationship of the moral and spiritual dimensions of Christian living. Catholic moral theology, under the influence of the philosophy of nominalism, gradually became focused on acts, rules, and casuistry rather than the broader Thomistic emphasis on virtues in the context of a striving to attain the ultimate end. Discussion of virtue was reduced almost to providing an organizing structure for discussing the sinful acts that "opposed" particular virtues. Catholic moral theology—all the way up to the manuals of moral theology in use before the Second Vatican Council—remained tied to and more akin with emphases in canon law than to dogmatic theology and spirituality.

Moral theology was still aimed formally and remotely at "perfection" and the ultimate end, but usually only by way of introduction and as a prelude to the discussion of individual human actions aimed at discrete ends. In fact, moral theology seemed more aimed at natural human ends, cut off from the sense of the moral life as part of the Christian response to God. Moral theology came to concern itself largely with the avoidance of sin, and following the commandments for the ordinary Christian. Spiritual theology, on the other hand, as a branch of the moral theology still formally directed to the ultimate end, focused on the moral life beyond the commandments and with the life of prayer, largely for a special elite corps of Christians from among the priests and religious. For many, moral theology became the realm of precepts and commandments that obliged all Christians, while spiritual theology was the realm of counsels for those few called to a special holiness.

The seventeenth and eighteenth centuries saw the further distinction within spiritual theology between ascetical and mystical theology. Ascetical theology concentrated on advance in virtue and on the first stages of prayer up to infused forms of contemplation. It retained, then, the moral dimension of the Christian life as a necessary aspect of growth in Christian life and prayer. Although ascetical theology focused attention on infused rather than acquired virtues, it preserved many aspects of the unity of the moral and spiritual life—even while moral theology, of which it was formally a branch, was reduced to a minimalism cut off from the biblical and patristic emphasis on the Christian life as radically transformed in Christ. Beyond ascetical theology, mystical theology studied the further development of Christian life and prayer beyond what could be attained by human effort aided by the normal working of grace. Mystical theology focused on infused forms of prayer which involved the closest approach to the beatific vision that could be attained in the present existence.[6]

The Three Ways—purgative, illuminative, and unitive—continued to structure many manuals of ascetical and mystical theology. In this way, ascetical and mystical theology continued the traditional insight concerning the necessity for a concurrent moral and spiritual growth. The ability of spiritual theology to retain this insight is perhaps rooted in the ongoing *experience* of mystics who reported that authentic spiritual growth demanded a true moral growth. Nowhere is this more clearly exemplified than in *The Ascent of Mount Carmel* by St. John of the Cross—upon which generations of ascetical and mystical writers would base their own examinations of the spiritual life. Sadly, the work of the ascetical and mystical writers was intended for a spiritual elite and was not to be recommended for the average Christian.

At least since the separation of theology into its specializations of moral and dogmatic theology, then, the relationship of moral theology and spirituality involved the subordination of the latter to the former.[7] Drawing its principles from dogmatic theology, spirituality aimed at directing a few special Christians to attain the heights of the Christian quest, nominally the goal of a more minimalistic moral theology. Although Pierre Pourrat, the author of the first modern history of spirituality, maintained the superiority of spirituality over moral theology,[8] Sandra Schneiders has argued that Pourrat's claims of superiority merely elevated spirituality even further to the level of an esoteric discipline disconnected from the lives of ordinary Christians.[9]

It is really the explicit recognition of the universal call to holiness by the Second Vatican Council (*Lumen gentium*, nos. 39–41) that has helped to break down and to overcome the dualism created by a two-tiered view of the Christian life—moral theology for the vast majority of average Christians, spirituality for an elite few. If every Christian life is aimed at union with God, then moral theology and spirituality should be interrelated perspectives on the development of the disciples' relationship with God. All Christians are called both to moral goodness and to authentic holiness.

The Contemporary Situation

The contemporary renewal of both Catholic moral theology and Christian spirituality seems to hold a good deal of promise in reaffirming the interconnection between moral and spiritual striving. Still, while there have been some important efforts to demonstrate the connection between these two disciplines,[10] a great deal more work and attention lies ahead. The present state of each discipline manifests both the promise and the ongoing challenge.

As we pointed out in the introduction, the Second Vatican Council challenged moral theology to return to its theological and biblical roots and to reclaim its more transcendent goal:

> Special care should be given to the perfecting of moral theology. Its scientific presentation should draw more fully on the teaching of Holy Scripture and should throw light upon the exalted vocation of the faithful in Christ and their obligation to bring forth charity for the life of the world.[11]

The response to this challenge has resulted in a contemporary moral theology more explicitly rooted in dogmatic theology and scripture, more personalist, more Christocentric, more ecumenically aware, and more concerned with social dimensions of morality. Prodded a bit by the recent Protestant emphasis on virtue and character associated especially with the work of Stanley Hauerwas, Catholic moral theology has begun to return to its Thomistic emphasis on virtue and thus to root moral theology in the broader tasks of Christian living.[12] The Christian moral life is understood more explicitly in the context of the Christian community and in its liturgy and its formative narratives—the very context which nurtures the spiritual life.

Perhaps foremost in the modern renewal of contemporary moral theology has been the work of the German moral theologian, Bernard Häring. Enda McDonagh has said of Häring's work:

> In the renewal of moral theology in which Father Häring's *The Law of Christ* proved such a seminal work, the artificial distinction between moral and ascetical theology and mystical theology was in principle overcome. The double standard of Christian living, symbolised by the precepts and counsels and to be realized by laity and religious, the less perfect and the perfect, gradually lost its significance.[13]

Häring's own work was fueled largely by the belief that there are two basic and inseparable forms of the human response to God's gratuitous self-offering: worship (both private and communal) and moral living.[14] The two responses cannot be separated in the lives of the individual Christian. Häring has devoted himself to the development of a faith-filled and prayer-nourished moral theology that has easily allowed him to cross over into numerous works on prayer, worship, and spirituality.

Many recent textbooks of fundamental moral theology make explicit reference to the important connection between moral theology and spirituality.[15] Still, the explicit effort to demonstrate the connection between the two dimensions of Christian existence and between the two disciplines is not extensive. Further, certain emphases in contemporary moral theology continue to mask or even impede our ability to see the connection between moral theology and spirituality. As McDonagh notes:

> Moral theology pays lip-service to its continuity with ascetical and mystical theology but in its literature and teaching continues to concern itself with the traditional moral areas, albeit in a new setting and with a new awareness of the positive open-ended character of the moral call. This is partly due to the inertia of history and tradition.[16]

Although McDonagh's comment is now some fifteen years old, it remains nonetheless largely accurate.

Contemporary Catholic moral theology continues to focus a great deal of attention on specific moral issues and on the methodologies used to address them. This important effort to address particular questions in social, medical, and sexual ethics necessitates a discussion of methodologies—such as the contemporary controverted discussion of proportionalism—for resolving these questions. This focus is certainly proper to moral theology's essential purposes, but it does tend to keep the attention of Catholic moral theology on acts. As Protestant ethicist James Gustafson has observed of contemporary Catholic ethics:

> My impression is that the traditional concentration of moral theology on acts is largely continued, and that those acts and their circumstances which have occupied attention for

religious reasons continue to receive dominant attention, e.g., war, sexuality, contraception, abortion, euthanasia, suicide. Thomas Aquinas' 'Treatise on Human Acts' seems always to be in the background.[17]

Within a focus on specific issues and methodologies, the discussion of the relationship between moral theology and spirituality can seem secondary, abstract, or even ethereal. In fact, however, an understanding of the relationship of ethics and spirituality provides the broad context which makes sense of the actions of Christians. The point, obviously, is not to neglect the important issues being discussed today; but, rather, to focus attention on the broader context as well. It is certainly a task proper to moral theology's essential purposes to help Christians to understand their actions and their moral striving within the broader purposes of the Christian life itself.

Another emphasis of contemporary Catholic moral theology also seems to divert attention away from the relationship of ethics and spirituality. This is the ongoing—and, again, very important—discussion of the "distinctiveness of Christian ethics." The Catholic moral tradition has always been a "natural law" tradition, believing that human reason is a reliable source for the formulation of moral norms. This emphasis on reason has been the basis for allowing the Catholic tradition to enter into moral dialogue with "people of good will" who do not share Christian faith. Such dialogue is especially important in pluralistic, largely secular contemporary societies. But the very presupposition that reason is a reliable source for the attainment of moral truth raises the question of the "distinctiveness of Christian ethics": if moral truth is attainable by reason, in what way is Christian faith necessary for Christian ethics? Different moral theologians have answered this question differently.

The purpose in pointing to the "distinctiveness of Christian ethics" debate is not to enter into the important questions it raises. It is certainly not our purpose to deny a natural law foundation for moral norms nor to deny that norms are "in principle" available to people who do not share Christian faith. It does seem, however, that the effort to reaffirm the natural law, reason-based foundation of moral norms can divert attention from non-rational foundations of Christian ethics. Furthermore, the effort to affirm that moral norms are "in principle" available to those without explicit Christian faith can distract from the equally important questions of *how* explicit Christian faith—as lived and celebrated by ordinary Christians—*does*, in fact, impact, form, and guide the Christian moral life. Finally, the vitally important task of dialogue on moral questions in a pluralistic society can divert attention from the essential *intra*-community task of helping committed Christians to make sense of their moral lives in light of their spiritual longing.

In short, while the contemporary, ongoing renewal of Catholic moral theology has largely reclaimed the discipline's theological and biblical foundations, the renewal has still not progressed to the point of manifesting the connection between moral and spiritual striving. It must be said, then, that Catholic moral theology is still cut off from the full dynamism of authentic Christian living. It does not yet fully reflect the actual lives of Christians who must pray in order to become truly good and who must become morally good in order to grow in prayer and in holiness.

For its part, contemporary Christian spirituality also seems to be in a state of fundamental reevaluation. It has clearly recognized and responded to the inadequacies of some aspects of pre–Vatican II spiritualities. John Heagle has suggested, for example, that pre–Vatican II spiritualities shared four problematic characteristics: (1) they were *theoretical* in their starting point—that is, largely deduced from doctrinal principles; (2) they were *elitist* in their assumptions—that is, directed only to certain priests and religious; (3) they were *other-worldly* in their perspectives—that is, suspicious and even hostile toward the present historical realities; and (4) they were *individualistic* in their practice—that is, detached from social concern and from an appreciation of the communal and liturgical dimensions of Christian life and spirituality.[18]

Contemporary literature in the academic discipline of spirituality suggests that there is, at present, a fundamental reevaluation of the appropriate terminology for and the definition of the discipline itself as well as a reevaluation of the scope and methods of the discipline.[19] The current preference by some authors for the term "spirituality," for example, to describe the discipline represents a disavowal of the term "spiritual theology," more traditional in Catholic circles. "Spirituality" seems to be more inclusive in its ability to incorporate *both* the religious experience of persons *and* the academic discipline which reflects on the experience. Further, "spirituality" seems better able to encompass the ecumenical and interreligious nature of the discipline and seems to distinguish it from the deductive approach of the earlier "spiritual theology" subordinated to dogmatic and moral theology.

Michael Downey has suggested that certain trends in contemporary spirituality are now identifiable, many of which seem to respond to some of the more problematic characteristics of pre–Vatican II spiritualities summarized by Heagle.[20] Among the ten trends identified by Downey, several hold immediate promise for fostering a more adequate relationship between spirituality and moral theology. Among these trends are: sustained attention to a more holistic understanding of spirituality; the effort to undercut any form of dualism which would excessively separate mundane life and activity from some "other-worldly" spiritual realm; the more interdisciplinary approach of spirituality; the conviction that prayer and action are two dimensions of the human person which must be held together; a greater awareness of the ecological impact of spiritualities; and the recognition of the need to retrieve the insights of the past. It would seem that these trends would naturally lead to a greater connection between the disciplines of moral theology and spirituality.

Beyond academic writings about spirituality, the popular literature of spirituality does not seem to manifest a great deal of attention to the relationship between moral and spiritual dimensions of Christian life—although, as Downey's trends suggest, there is a recognition that prayer and action cannot be separated. Contemporary ecological spiritualities[21] alluded to by Downey and discussions of spirituality and social justice[22] do suggest a unity between any authentic spirituality and the person's being in the world. By their very nature, of course, the developing liberation spiritualities presuppose that any authentic Christian spirituality is vitally connected with the sociopolitical dimensions of life.[23]

In sum, the contemporary, ongoing reevaluation and renewal of Christian spirituality as an academic discipline seems to hold great promise for a greater integration with moral theology. Still, it may be that contemporary spirituality must, at present, focus on its own internal questions before it can pursue this integration with moral theology more fully. At the same time, however, the continuing renewal of spirituality may be furthered by conscious attention to its foundational connection with moral theology.

Suggestions for the Future

Both Catholic moral theology and Christian spirituality continue their ongoing renewal and development as distinct theological disciplines. The purpose of the historical and contemporary sketch that occupied most of this chapter is not meant to suggest that they should somehow return to a simpler bygone era before they became distinct disciplines. It is obvious that each has its own legitimate and important focus.

This sketch has suggested, however, that the authentic further development of each discipline requires more than passing laudatory mention of the other. Both our moral and spiritual traditions and the continuing lived experience of Christians reveals that the Christian moral life is nurtured by a vibrant spiritual life and that authentic spiritual development cannot occur without a concurrent moral development. In order for each discipline to fulfill its ecclesial, pastoral purpose of nourishing and guiding Christian living, it will be necessary to pursue an explicit and ongoing dialogue between the disciplines and mutual incorporation of the insights of each. At least five broad suggestions seem to follow from the historical development and contemporary state of both disciplines.

First, Catholic moral theology must continue to reclaim the broader and even transcendent context provided by its relationship with spirituality. Moral theology cannot be restricted to norms and decision-making—nor even to virtue and character. Moral theology serves the Christian life aimed at sharing together in the divine life of the Trinity—a life with our sisters and brothers in triune community. The Christian life is a radically new life in Christ, conformed to Christ, transformed in Christ. It is then a life animated by charity, empowered by the indwelling Spirit, aimed at sharing in triune love. The trinitarian focus of moral theology points to the important social dimension of both moral theology and spirituality. The authentic life of persons created in the image of a triune and personal God cannot ignore the needs and demands of other persons in the human community.

Second, contemporary moral theology must continue to point to the Christian moral life as empowered by grace, made possible only by God's gracious presence and action in individual Christians, in the Christian community, and in the world. Moral theology must therefore recover what the tradition discussed as "infused virtue" (moral and theological), and charity as the "form" of the virtues and thus of the moral life—a love empowered by and ultimately directed toward God. It is only in this transcendent and grace-filled context that discussions of virtue, natural law, norms, acts, and decision-making can make sense as *Christian* ethics. Otherwise moral theology will continue the bifurcation of the moral life from the spiritual life and thus fail to provide authentic and holistic guidance to Christian men and women struggling to become both good and holy.

Third, for its part, contemporary spirituality cannot lose touch with the insights discussed in the traditional treatises on ascetical theology. The foundation of sustained spiritual growth in moral growth is a clear presupposition, not only of our own spiritual tradition but also of the mystical traditions of every major religion. Any authentic growth in prayer, contemplation, and mysticism requires overcoming sin and growth in moral goodness. Any spirituality that proposes a "quick road" to the heights of prayer (or even to an authentic, sustained life of prayer) without attention to moral conversion is both inauthentic to our tradition and alien to our experience. This requires that contemporary spirituality recover notions of purgation and asceticism that are authentically and appropriately world-affirming and creation-serving and that guide Christian women and men in the integration of all of their desires into their striving after God.

Fourth, the ongoing renewal of Christian spirituality seems well-served by the contemporary discipline's attention to experience. The most fundamental human experience which is the focus of both spirituality and moral theology is the drive to authentic self-transcendence, in prayer and in action. As Schneiders reviews the current efforts to arrive at a common definition for "spirituality," she argues that "virtually everyone talking about spirituality these days is talking about self-transcendence which gives integrity and meaning to the whole of life and to life in its wholeness by situating and orienting the person within the horizon of ultimacy in some ongoing and transforming way." In this context, she defines Christian spirituality as "that particular actualization of the capacity for self-transcendence that is constituted by the substantial gift of the Holy Spirit establishing a life-giving relationship with God in Christ within the believing community."[24]

Both Christian spirituality and moral theology focus on and ultimately seek to serve the authentic self-transcendence in love which is at the heart of both true prayer and moral living. Such self-transcendence in prayer and in Christian living, modelled on the death and resurrection of Jesus, is the ongoing task of the Christian life as a whole. But this is but another way of saying that ongoing and continual conversion is the task of Christian living. It is perhaps the experience of conversion itself—both as a critical moment in the lives of many Christians but also the ongoing, continual conversion of Christians—that offers a most fruitful place to rediscover the unity of moral and spiritual striving. This is the topic of the next chapter.

Fifth, building on a foundation in experience, moral theology and spirituality might usefully develop a common language to discuss such realities as their foundational experiences, the authentic development of mature human and

Christian living, and the supports and hindrances to that development. Moral theology and Christian spirituality do remain distinct disciplines with different objects and methods; still, they offer different perspectives on distinct aspects of the one Christian life. Thus, while each will necessarily develop its own distinctive vocabulary, they should speak a language which allows for clear and sustained interchange between the disciplines.

Conclusion

The contemporary recognition of the universal call to holiness must mean more than that the subject matter of the old manuals of ascetical and mystical theology is now for the laity. Surely it must mean that every Christian is called to moral goodness rooted in an openness to the divine initiative and action through prayer and aimed at a share in the divine life itself. Every Christian, then, is called to a life grounded in conversion, rooted in community, empowered by grace, and aimed at communion with God and with others in God. All Christians are called to the life of ongoing self-transcendence in a continual conversion that seeks to manifest the unity of love of God and of neighbor. If contemporary Catholic moral theology and Christian spirituality are to help Christians to respond to this universal call to holiness, then they must attend to one another in an explicit and sustained way and they must speak a common language that challenges and guides people to become both good and holy.

The Dynamism of the Christian Life

2

CONVERSION AT THE HEART OF CHRISTIAN LIFE

It would be difficult to argue that the notion of conversion has been in any way central to the explicit development of the academic disciplines of spirituality and moral theology, at least until recently. Not so many years ago, "conversion," in Roman Catholic circles, usually meant either entering the Catholic Church from some other religious tradition, or simply turning away from sin. Clearly, the *notion* of conversion has only begun to play an important role in the ongoing development of the academic disciplines of moral theology and spirituality; however, the *experience* of conversion has nonetheless always been central to the development of the Christian life, both morally and spiritually. In fact, the unity of Christian moral and spiritual striving—and of the disciplines that study them—is grounded precisely in conversion, both as decision and commitment and as further integration and deepening.

Christian conversion is the total—if never entirely complete—surrender of the person to God as revealed in Jesus Christ. Christian conversion, as the continual process of self-surrender to God in Christ, therefore encompasses every aspect of the Christian life and necessarily grounds the moral and spiritual efforts of every Christian. In many ways, the chapters that follow will simply specify the shape of this ongoing conversion in the various aspects of the Christian life.

My presentation in this chapter will proceed in the following way: First, we will examine the relationship of religious conversion to other forms of conversion. It will be apparent that my analysis is dependent on the work of Bernard Lonergan in dialogue with the work of Walter Conn. Second, we will discuss the relationship between religious conversion in general and Christian conversion in particular. Third, we will explicate the way in which Christian conversion grounds the whole of the Christian life and certainly the Christian's moral and spiritual efforts. Fourth, we will discuss the implications of the fact that conversion to Christ is also conversion to the reign of God that Jesus came to announce. Fifth, we will examine conversion as an ongoing, continual process in the Christian life. Finally, we will conclude with some summary remarks about conversion and the unity of morality and spirituality. As will be apparent, our purpose is to examine conversion as the foundation of the unity of morality and spirituality rather than to attempt a comprehensive theology of Christian conversion.[1]

Religious Conversion and Other Forms of Conversion

Bernard Lonergan has provided important insights into conversion and into the various types of conversion.[2] Other theologians have furthered his analyses of the experience of conversion itself and of conversion as foundational for theology.[3] For our present purposes, we will focus in particular on religious conversion as it relates to other forms of conversion—that is, how "other-worldly falling in love" flows out into the moral and spiritual lives of Christians.

For Lonergan, conversion is rooted in the inherent human drive for self-transcendence. The experience of conversion itself involves a radical shift in horizons, in the perspective from which the person views reality itself. It is therefore a transformation of the person and of his or her world, a transcending of self and of one's view of reality.[4] As lived, conversion "affects all of a man's conscious and intentional operations. It directs his gaze, pervades his imagination, releases the symbols that penetrate to the depths of his psyche. It enriches his understanding, guides his judgments, reinforces his decisions."[5] A very brief review of the types of conversion identified by Lonergan and others will provide the necessary background for our discussion.

For Lonergan, intellectual conversion involves the transformation of the person as knowing subject through the elimination of the myth that all knowing is simply like looking. The person who has experienced intellectual conversion has come to see that knowing is more than seeing; it involves experiencing, understanding, judging, and believing.[6]

Moral conversion involves the transformation of the person as an agent. The person who has been morally converted no longer bases decisions on the effort to attain mere satisfactions; rather, the morally converted individual begins to act for the sake of authentic values, especially the value of persons and their needs. The morally converted are able to choose for the attainment of value even when the value conflicts with the possible attainment of present satisfaction.[7]

It must be noted that moral conversion aims at self-transcendence for values over mere satisfaction not only on occasion but habitually; that is, moral conversion is directed not only at intermittent good choices but rather at the virtuous character habitually disposed to make good choices. As Conn states: "But it is one thing to transcend oneself in response to value once in a while. It is another to do it consistently. Only after many years of development does there emerge in the conscious human subject the *sustained* self-transcendence of the virtuous person."[8]

Lonergan does not offer an explicit discussion of affective conversion in *Method in Theology*. Although Lonergan discusses it in later works, others have developed the understanding of affective conversion more thoroughly. Stephen Happel and James J. Walter define affective conversion as "a modality of self-transcendence in which we move from narcissistic love to a self-giving love of others."[9] Conn describes it as a "dynamic state of being-in-love," in which the person no longer acts for self but for others.[10]

Affective conversion plays an important role in empowering and sustaining moral conversion.[11] The affectively converted person acts not merely for the sake of the values *associated* with persons but rather for the sake of real persons as neighbors and as unique gifts. In so doing, affective conversion gives the affective power and drive, the passion and commitment, to sustain moral conversion in its drive to become habitual, even in the face of serious obstacles.[12]

Religious conversion, for Lonergan, "is an other-worldly falling in love. It is total and permanent self-surrender without conditions, qualifications, reservations. But it is such a surrender, not as an act, but as a dynamic state that is prior to and principle of subsequent acts."[13] Once a person has experienced religious conversion, their "other-worldly falling in love" becomes the principle of all choice and action. We can see, therefore, that religious conversion becomes the principle, the beginning, of all moral and spiritual effort.

In Lonergan's order of presentation, the conversions progress from intellectual to moral, to affective, and finally to religious conversion. Each conversion is related to the earlier conversion by "sublation," which is to say that a later conversion "takes up" and "includes" the previous conversion, adding new elements but destroying nothing of the earlier conversion.[14] Each is a different modality of the human drive for self-transcendence.

Lonergan's initial presentation of the types of conversion can seem to suggest a *linear* development that moves from intellectual to moral, through affective, and finally to religious conversion, with each previous conversion sublated by the latter. But, as Lonergan himself goes on to observe, in the causal order and in the order of experience, normally there is religious conversion that flows out into others:

> Though religious conversion sublates moral, and moral conversion sublates intellectual, one is not to infer that intellectual comes first and then moral and finally religious. On the contrary, from a causal viewpoint, one would say that first there is God's gift of love. Next, the eye of this love reveals values in their splendor, while the strength of this love brings about their realization, and that is moral conversion. Finally, among the values discerned by the eye of love is the value of believing the truths taught by religious

tradition, and in such tradition and belief are the seeds of intellectual conversion.[15]

Thus, even if the adult convert has previously experienced a moral or intellectual conversion, these will be so radically transformed in religious conversion that they seem to flow out as new from the religious conversion. As Lonergan says, religious conversion "dismantles and abolishes the horizon in which our knowing and choosing went on and it sets up a new horizon in which the love of God will transvalue our values and the eyes of that love will transform our knowing."[16] Religious conversion flows out into the other conversions; and, although it does not necessitate the experience of affective, moral, and intellectual conversion, religious conversion seeks to be realized more completely through the other conversions. For our present purposes it will be helpful to suggest some ways in which religious conversion flows over into the other conversions.

Religious conversion as an "other-worldly falling in love" rather naturally pours forth into love for other persons. It gives the person an even greater passion and commitment for acting on behalf of others rather than merely for the self. Religious conversion, therefore, encourages and then strengthens and deepens affective conversion. When religious conversion is more particularly a Christian conversion, there is further explicit empowerment for love of neighbor since Jesus has inseparably linked the love of God and love of neighbor.

We have already seen that affective conversion enables the person to overcome moral impotence and sustain the self-transcendence entailed in acting for values over satisfactions. The unrestricted love of religious conversion further empowers moral conversion by transforming the depth and the breadth of one's loving. Further, religious conversion gives new reasons to choose values, since these values reflect God as the source of all values. As Lonergan says, "the eye of love reveals values in their splendor," so that authentic values are seen more clearly. Religious conversion impacts moral conversion as a "transvaluing of our valuing."

Finally, religious conversion encourages intellectual conver-

sion, since it drives one to understand one's other-worldly falling
in love. In short, it makes one a theologian, and it becomes
apparent very quickly that this task cannot be adequately
accomplished solely by empirical knowing or "common sense."[17]

Brian Johnstone has suggested that the process of transformation begun in religious conversion and flowing out into the
rest be understood as a spiral rather than in linear fashion:

> Perhaps the process of integral transformation should be
> envisaged not so much as a linear, temporal sequence of
> religious, moral, intellectual, but rather as a spiral where a
> deepening religious transformation tends (allowing for
> limitations of individuals) to draw forth a deepening moral
> and a deepening intellectual conversion.[18]

In any case, it is clear that the outpouring of God's gift of love and
the human response in religious conversion become the dynamic
source of every aspect of the Christian's life—including, of course,
both morality and spirituality.

Religious Conversion and Christian Conversion

Christian conversion is the form that religious conversion
takes when it occurs through the appropriation of the Christian
story, that is, when Jesus Christ becomes the normative foundation for understanding God, self, others, and the world.[19]
Therefore, all that has been said in the previous section
concerning the impact of religious conversion on the other
conversions applies directly to Christian conversion, although in
a distinctively Christian way. The meaning and implications of
the distinctiveness of Christian conversion will be further
explicated in the section that follows, but first it will be helpful to
clarify the relationship between religious conversion in general
and Christian conversion in particular.

Walter Conn makes a clear distinction between Christian
conversion and religious conversion. Christian conversion is an
authentic transformation that may establish one on the path to
religious conversion, but it is not yet a true religious conversion.[20]
Ultimately, I will suggest that Conn's distinction is overstated,

but I believe that examination of his position will highlight the meaning of Christian conversion itself and its ongoing nature.

For Conn, Christian conversion is the transformation involved when one enters into relationship with God in the person of Jesus Christ. While arguing that Christian conversion is more than moral conversion, Conn considers it to be "one particular way moral conversion is realized concretely in individual lives in terms of very specific personal and communal values."[21] Religious conversion, on the other hand, has a more radical character; it is, as Lonergan had earlier defined it, total and without qualification or reserve. Conn says:

> But if Christian conversion is more than moral conversion, it is also less than religious conversion as I have defined it here. Just as not all Christians have experienced Christian conversion, not all who have experienced the transformation of a relationship with Christ have experienced the radical falling-in-love with God that is religious conversion.[22]

Thus, for Conn, Christian conversion is far more than mere nominal adherence to Christianity, but it is a relatively more common experience in the life of committed Christians. Religious conversion, on the other hand, is relatively rare because of its totality. Conn believes that true religious conversion may be best understood as more closely connected with mystical experience than with the normal experience of even genuinely committed Christians.[23]

I would suggest that Conn overstates the distinction between Christian and religious conversion. Lonergan himself makes the distinction between being in love in an "unrestricted" manner "as defined" and "as achieved." The *achievement* of this unrestricted being in love that is at the heart of religious conversion actually occurs "dialectically"—"never complete and always precarious."[24] In short, Lonergan does not argue that the actual experience of religious conversion involves the *already completely realized* character of love without reservation or qualification. In fact, for Lonergan to do so would imply that all conversion-based theology would be grounded in relatively rare mystical experience. While a good case could be made for the unwarranted neglect of mystical experience as a theological source in contemporary Catholic theology,[25] it does not seem that Lonergan himself is arguing that conversion-based theology is grounded in mystical experience but rather in the genuine religious conversion that is more widely experienced but aiming at the mystical.

I would certainly agree that not every Christian has, in fact, experienced Christian conversion, since Christian conversion is far more than mere nominal adherence to Christianity. It seems to me, however, that any authentic Christian conversion does involve a nascent "other-worldly falling in love," a true *intention* and *commitment* to the complete totality of self-surrender to God. As such, it involves a quality of total commitment, a true transformation of the person and not a mere change or development. Converted Christians surrender themselves wholly if not yet completely. The "achievement" of this unrestricted and total love is, as Lonergan suggests, the result of graced effort over a lifetime—which points precisely to the ongoing and continual character of Christian conversion to be discussed below.

Perhaps we might understand the religious "falling in love" entailed in a genuine Christian conversion after an analogy with marital love. The love of newlyweds for one another can be romantic, naive, and quite incomplete. In order to mature, it must perdure over time and face sacrifice, hardship and struggle. And yet even this romantic and naive love may be truly authentic love, the nascent form of the mature love that will eventually become the more complete union of fully adult husband and wife. The loving self-giving of newlyweds can be "total" without yet being complete. In the same way, the being in love of the only recently converted Christian may be naive and romantic in its own way; it must be matured by hardship and sacrifice (that is, by embracing the cross); and yet it can still be true religious conversion that aims at the completeness that presently exists in the Christian as a potential and a hope.

Authentic Christian conversion, then, is the Christian form of authentic religious conversion; and the radical self-abandonment to God of the mystic is a profoundly "deeper" integration or more complete realization of the self-surrender first offered in the Christian conversion itself. Continual Christian conversion, including the graced effort to grow in both goodness and holiness, is the dynamism of an authentic other-worldly falling in love seeking its penultimate accomplishment in a mystical self-surrender.

Conversion to Christ and Christian Living

Conversion to Christ sets the convert on a distinctively Christian way of life—on "The Way," as the early Christians referred quite simply to their faith and manner of living. Conversion to Christ, then, establishes the Christian on the path of a distinctively Christian moral and spiritual striving. It involves growing in a relationship of loving response to God, accepting and internalizing the Christian story as normative for one's life, and the conforming of one's life to that of Christ.

Christian conversion is not just a new way of seeing but a new way of being because one has entered into a radically new relationship with God in Christ. Conversion to Christ is a response to the outpouring of God's love and the grateful acceptance of the friendship that God offers to sinners. It is a response empowered by Christ through the Spirit and modelled after the life, death, and resurrection of Jesus. Bernard Häring argues that this grateful and loving response of the Christian takes two basic forms: worship/prayer (spirituality) and moral living (morality).[26] Every experience of conversion as well as every effort at ongoing conversion is a response to God's gratuitous initiative.

The response of the Christian that follows upon conversion is grounded in the Christian story, most especially in the life, teaching, death, and resurrection of Jesus. The Christian story becomes normative for the Christian's life, because he or she comes to accept this story as the most credible interpretation of life's meaning and purpose. Christian conversion, then, brings a transformed vision and a transformed way of being. Especially within the context of the Christian community, the Christian internalizes the Christian story through reading and study, through meditation on the scriptures, through prayer, through the living witnesses of saints and fellow Christians, and through the celebration of the liturgy. Gradually, the transformed vision of Christian conversion deepens the transformation of the Christian himself or herself so that he or she develops distinctively Christian perspectives, dispositions, affections, intentions, priorities. These distinctively Christian elements lead to the development of the Christian character and inform every act of understanding, judgment, and decision that the Christian makes in his or her daily life.

It is clear that Christian conversion brings, not merely an external imitation of Christ, but a deepening conforming of one's life to that of Christ. The Christian identifies with Christ as the living source of communion with God. The person who has experienced Christian conversion is, in New Testament terms, "in Christ," a "new person in Christ," a "new creation in Christ." Conformity to Christ, then, means to live as he lived: "By this we may be sure that we are in him: whoever says 'I abide in him,' ought to walk just as he walked" (1 Jn 2:5–6). Frank Fletcher, reflecting on Lonergan's discussion of discipleship as a "mutual self-mediation in Christ," maintains that Christian discipleship must be understood as a "mutuality in praxis" between the disciple and Jesus.[27] Further, the Christian's conformity to Christ means to think like Christ and to share his attitudes: "Let the same mind be in you that was in Christ Jesus..." (Phil 2:5). Ultimately, conformity to Christ means becoming so conformed to Christ that one can say with St. Paul that one's life is "hidden with Christ in God" (Col 3:3), or "I have been crucified with Christ; and it is no longer I, but Christ who lives in me" (Gal 2:19–20).

Christian conversion as conformity to Christ and setting out on the path of discipleship necessarily involves the personal appropriation of the paschal mystery.[28] In short, Christian conversion, and the path of ongoing conversion on which it establishes a person, involves a conformity to the cross. Like Jesus, the disciple seeks a continual self-giving in a world of limit and of sin. Embracing the cross involves the acceptance of suffering that cannot be avoided, the sometimes painful self-surrender entailed in loving service of others, the taking up of the discipline that a sustained life of prayer requires, the acceptance of the purgation that advancing prayer brings, and the self-sacrifice involved in courageous action on behalf of justice. Conversion to Christ, and therefore the authentic moral and spiritual lives of his disciples, means the taking up of one's cross in joyful expectation of the resurrection.

Conversion to the Reign of God

Conversion to Christ is necessarily conversion to the reign of God that he came to proclaim and to inaugurate.[29] In the gospel of Mark (1:15), Jesus challenges the people to repentance, to conversion, *because* "the time is fulfilled, and the kingdom of God has come near."[30] Encounter with the reign of God, most especially in the person of Jesus, challenges the person to make a decision in the here and now, for or against Christ, for or against God's reign. Jim Wallis has stated this point most emphatically:

> Jesus inaugurated a new age, heralded a new order, and called the people to conversion. "Repent!" he said. Why? Because the new order of the kingdom is breaking in upon you and, if you want to be a part of it, you will need to undergo a fundamental transformation. Jesus makes the need for conversion clear from the beginning. God's new order is so radically different from everything we are accustomed to that we must be spiritually remade before we are ready and equipped to participate in it....No aspect of human existence is safe from this sweeping change— neither the personal, nor the spiritual, social, economic, and political.[31]

Because Christian conversion is always conversion to the reign of God, it can never be understood in an individualistic way. God's reign involves calling people together into authentic relationships that conform to God's loving will and purposes. God's reign is directed to the final ingathering of all men and women into the mutual self-giving of trinitarian life. Therefore, since the Christian moral and spiritual lives are grounded in conversion to Christ and to the reign of God, they can never be understood authentically in a privatized or individualistic way.

Further, conversion to Christ and to God's reign means conversion to God's purposes for the world and to the reign of God as it is breaking even now into human history. The reign of God is manifested in the world wherever love and justice are concretely, if imperfectly, realized in personal, interpersonal, structural, and global relationships. Christian conversion, then, includes a sociopolitical dimension, and it involves a commitment to justice at its core and not just as a derivative effect. Donald Gelpi therefore speaks of a distinct "socio-political conversion" that authenticates but de-privatizes intellectual, moral, affective, and religious conversions.[32]

Any view of the Christian life that neglects the challenges of God's reign in the present historical moment must be firmly rejected. It is precisely the dualistic separation of human history from God's reign that resulted in a minimalistic "this-worldly" Christian morality without a transcendent vision and an elitist and excessively "other-worldly" Christian spirituality that viewed involvement for justice as derivative or secondary. Contemporary Catholic moral theology and Christian spirituality are both actively rejecting these aberrations and, in doing so, are manifesting their relationship with one another. Christian conversion means conversion to the reign of God breaking into human history, and any authentically Christian morality or spirituality must attend to this inbreaking.

Conversion to the reign of God means conversion to the community that heralds God's reign, the church.[33] Faith comes to the Christian from the church's witness and testimony to the reign of God. The church provides the symbols, the stories, the language, and the concepts that allow the conversion to be celebrated, made explicit, and carried forward. It is the life of the church that supports, nurtures, and guides the ongoing conversion of the Christian. It is the church, precisely as a community rather than as merely isolated persons, that can give powerful witness to the inbreaking of God's reign. In a later chapter, we will look more particularly at the vital role that the church's liturgy in particular plays in the ongoing conversion of the Christian.

Donald Gelpi summarizes the importance of recognizing conversion as commitment to the reign of God:

> In other words, the initial consent of faith transforms one into a disciple of Jesus committed to his vision of the kingdom, concerned to submit to its moral demands in all one's personal decisions, and committed to laboring as the instrument of God in transforming human society according to the moral demands of life in God's kingdom.[34]

Conversion as a Continual Process

Bernard Lonergan discusses conversion as continual in terms of the traditional distinction between operative and cooperative grace:

> Operative grace is the replacement of the heart of stone by a heart of flesh, a replacement beyond the horizon of the heart of stone. Cooperative grace is the heart of flesh becoming effective in good works through human freedom. Operative grace is religious conversion. Cooperative grace is the effectiveness of conversion, the gradual movement towards a full and complete transformation of the whole of one's living and feeling, one's thoughts, words, deeds, and omissions.[35]

It is in the context of this "gradual movement towards a full and complete transformation" that the daily struggle to grow in the moral and spiritual life can be understood.

The Christian tradition has long understood the attainment of spiritual and moral "perfection" to be a lifelong task, always initiated and empowered by grace. The metaphor of "journey" is a long-standing and consistent theme in the tradition for describing the dynamic character of the Christian spiritual life.[36] The traditional notion of the "Three Ways" of purgation, illumination, and union presupposes this dynamic growth in the Christian life, both morally and spiritually. The Eastern Christian tradition views the Christian life as a path of deification (*theosis*—

coming to share in the divine nature) in which the image of God present in the person but obscured by sin is transformed into the very likeness of God. Many contemporary Catholic moral theologians speak of the ongoing growth of the Christian life in terms of fundamental option. Subsequent chapters will focus on the Three Ways, *theosis*, and fundamental option as these specify ongoing conversion and reveal the inner unity of morality and spirituality.

Bernard Häring has long argued that the Christian moral life must be understood as a continual conversion. In particular, he has focused on the dynamic nature of conversion by linking it with the ongoing deepening and integration of the positive fundamental option. The positive fundamental option involves a dynamic orientation, self-disposing, of one's life to God. The fundamental option is strengthened and solidified through good choices, and ultimately it seeks to integrate all of one's choices into one's most fundamental "choice" for God. This dynamic integration of the fundamental option coincides with ongoing Christian conversion.[37]

Josef Fuchs also relates conversion to the positive fundamental option, and in that context he specifies more particularly what continual conversion entails. *Conversio continua*, he argues, occurs in three forms: "1) the radical neo-conversion, 2) continuous verification of one's self-gift to God, and 3) conversion from venial sin."[38] A brief explanation of each of these aspects will serve to further explicate the meaning of continual conversion.

In "radical neo-conversion," a person who has already committed oneself to love God in an enduring fashion "substantially deepens the intensity of his option for Christ and God." This might occur, for example, in an intense retreat experience. There is a genuine element of newness in this neo-conversion, since the person does experience a deeper self-realization or, we might say, a deeper appropriation of an earlier conversion.

The second form of continual conversion identified by Fuchs is a "continuous verification of our self-giving to Christ and to God." The Christian, through the good choices and acts of daily living, verifies his or her self-identity as a disciple and integrates his or her fundamental disposing of self to God. These acts of verification and integration bring a genuine growth in the Christian life and a maturing in love.

The third form of continual conversion involves the "conversion from venial sin." Turning from venial sin seems to be the reverse of the previous form of *conversio continua*. By turning from venial sin, the Christian turns from actions that are inconsistent with his or her disposing of self to God. This is the negative form of the "continuous verification of one's self-giving" in which the Christian chooses and acts in a manner consistent with, and which furthers, his or her self-disposing to God. It might be noted that the focused effort to overcome venial sin was an important aspect of the "illuminative way" as the dedicated Christian grows in virtue and in prayer.

Walter Conn has argued that, since Christian conversion is always a conscious and deliberate choice and commitment, continual conversion and fundamental option are closely related but not to be identified.[39] Fuchs, on the other hand, notes that Christian conversion includes some aspects that are available to reflexive consciousness but other aspects that are not:

> Hence, once again, conversion is always on the level where a person is present to himself, where you *cannot* fully reflect on it. Consequently, in conversion we are conscious that we are converting, that we are moving from sin to a love of God above all else. I cannot love God without knowing it; as a subject I am aware and conscious of it but this love of God is not an object of reflection. For full reflection is impossible. It would mean that I would have to go out of myself; when that occurs I as a whole am not present to myself. I cannot go out of myself and with conceptual clarity and certainty know that I am living in grace. True conversion occurs in the subject as subject, not as object of reflection.[40]

Finally, it must be noted that ongoing conversion occurs within the context of normal stages of moral and faith development, as the work of Walter Conn has made clear. While Christian conversion cannot be identified with natural stages in the process of human development, it must be acknowledged that Christian conversion in the life of individual Christians must be understood in relationship with this natural process of development. Certainly the grace of conversion can be mediated by natural human structures of development without simply being reduced to them.

Conclusion

The unity of moral and spiritual striving is grounded in their common foundation in the experience of Christian conversion. The Christian strives to become both good and holy in response to God's gracious self-offering in Christ. Because Christians have discovered that God has first loved them in Christ, so they are empowered to love God in return (1 Jn 4:10, 19). The "other-worldly falling in love" of Christian conversion, although incomplete and not yet perfectly realized, seeks a total self-surrender to God without qualification or restriction. And so, Christian conversion establishes the person on a lifetime path of surrendering to God, of integrating all of life's choices and actions into one's loving self-disposing to God, of conforming oneself to the self-giving of God revealed in Jesus Christ.

The moral and spiritual life of Christians flows from the graced effort to live out one's Christian conversion. It involves the ongoing self-giving of Christians who themselves celebrate the self-giving of God in Christ. The moral and spiritual efforts of Christians, then, are distinct but inseparable aspects of their continual conversion. The effort to become morally good and to perform right actions, together with the effort to grow in authentic relationships with God and with others, nurture and support—in fact, constitute—the ongoing conversion of Christians.

Moral theology and Christian spirituality, as the disciplines that study the moral and spiritual quest of Christians, necessarily flow from reflection on the experience of conversion. The authentic development of these disciplines and their ability to address adequately the lived experience of Christian men and women require each discipline to attend to the other, beginning at their source. The failure of moral theology and spirituality to enrich and to critique one another will make them even more remote from the actual lives of Christian people; it will cut them off from the rich accumulated wisdom of the Christian tradition itself; and their separation is likely to perpetuate the reduction of moral theology to moral problem-solving and the trivializing of spirituality to disembodied discussions of prayer and/or mundane attention to holistic health.

3

DYNAMISM AND INTEGRATION: FUNDAMENTAL OPTION AND THE THREE WAYS

The Christian life is most basically a lifelong response to God's gracious self-offer in Christ. The shape of this response is in many ways utterly personal to each believer; and, yet, in all believers the response of faith takes the basic shape of worship and moral living. Both in the personal worship of prayer and in the communal worship of liturgy and sacrament, the Christian responds to God in wonder, in gratitude, and in adoration. So, too, in the moral life, Christians strive to become the kinds of people and to perform the kinds of actions which are in line with the divine self-offering made manifest in Christ and conformed to the response which Jesus himself made to the Father. The life of prayer and moral living are thus two aspects of the one response which the Christian makes to God in and through Christ. Each involves a dynamic process, a growth that requires a lifetime of effort to cooperate with God's grace. In each, the person seeks to transcend self through love of God and love of neighbor, leading ultimately to a complete self-offering to the Father after the manner of Jesus.

The unity of our spiritual and moral striving as well as their dynamism have been made clear in the traditional understanding of the Three Ways of purgation, illumination, union. Growth in prayer and the effort to grow in communion with God require a concomitant struggle against vice and a growth in virtue. So much are the two interrelated that one cannot grow in prayer without a concurrent moral conversion—while any true moral conversion itself requires the gracious presence of God nurtured in prayer.

The present chapter seeks to further the examination of the Three Ways and thus of the relationship of the moral and spiritual life through the concept of the fundamental option. Fundamental option theory has most generally been used to provide a revised understanding of sin. Although its proponents have suggested that it can further explicate the nature of positive growth in the Christian life, few have demonstrated how this might be the case. In the present chapter, we will seek to explicate one way in which fundamental option theory can enlighten Christian living in a positive way.

It will be apparent that the discussion of both fundamental option theory and the Three Ways is closely related to ongoing conversion, discussed in the previous chapter. Both presuppose and examine the shape of authentic growth as a dynamic process in the Christian life. Both presuppose that growth as a Christian is inescapably moral and spiritual. Both, then, are different ways—one of them, contemporary, and the other, traditional—of examining the meaning of ongoing Christian conversion.

The Fundamental Option

Fundamental option theory has developed in Catholic moral theology as part of an effort to renew a Roman Catholic theology of sin.[1] The manuals of moral theology in use in seminary education before the Second Vatican Council placed an overemphasis on an understanding of sin as an act and as violation of law. In response to this overemphasis, Catholic moral theologians have attempted to develop an understanding of sin which is more relational, more biblically based, and more cognizant of psychological insights into personal and moral development and of philosophical reflections on the nature of human freedom. A complete discussion of fundamental option

theory obviously cannot be undertaken here, but a brief overview of its basic lines seems essential.

The basic insight of fundamental option theory is the
realization that sin and grace must be understood not primarily
in terms of individual acts for good or evil, but in light of the
person's basic life orientation or direction. The fundamental
option, whether positive or negative, is a response to the innate
human desire for God at our deepest core and to God's offer of
love in Christ—at a level not fully available to our consciousness.
The negative fundamental option—sin—is a life directed away
from God, a refusal of God's self-offer, and thus a contradiction of
the deepest desire and purpose of the human spirit. The positive
fundamental option—the life of grace—is a life directed toward
God, a living acceptance of the God of Jesus Christ. The
fundamental option, then, points to a dynamism in the Christian
life which may be better captured by the terms "fundamental
direction" or "fundamental orientation" than "option" or
"stance."

Fundamental option theory has been developed in a
number of different ways. Bernard Häring, for example, uses the
insights of developmental and depth psychology to enhance the
biblical notion of the "heart" as the deepest core of the person
where conversion and a growing relationship with God must
take place.[2] Joseph Fuchs builds more explicitly on the Thomistic
understanding of the human person ordered to God as ultimate
end as the foundation for a fundamental option theory.[3] The
traditional definition of sin as "a turning away from God and a
turning toward creatures" (*aversio a Deo per conversionem ad
creaturam*) then serves as a basis for understanding sin as a
negative fundamental option. Other theologians have developed
Karl Rahner's distinction between transcendental and
categorical freedom as the foundation for a distinction between a
fundamental level of freedom and the level of free choice(s).[4]

For Rahner, human freedom is not in the first instance a
freedom to choose among a variety of discrete objects—what we
usually call freedom of choice, or what we may refer to as
"categorical freedom." Rather, freedom is most basically the
capacity to decide about oneself. Freedom, at this transcendental

level, is ultimately the innate human capacity for a "yes" or "no" to God. The constitutive core of the person is this capacity to accept the divine self-offering; and it is the very purpose of freedom, under the influence of grace, to choose God. To surrender oneself freely and totally to God is freedom's truest purpose. As St. Augustine would have it, there are only two possible loves for us, the love of God to the forgetfulness of self, or the love of self to the forgetfulness of God.

The actualization of this transcendental freedom is not present to us as are the free choices we make throughout each day. Unlike the affirmative and negative responses we make to the choices available to us in our everyday life, our most basic "yes" or "no" to God is not fully available to our reflexive consciousness—that is, it is not fully available to our self-reflection. This is so because we cannot fully step "outside" ourselves to examine our deepest core. Furthermore, the "action" of transcendental freedom is not one act among others—just as God is not just one more object of choice among other, created, goods.

Although transcendental freedom cannot simply be equated with individual acts of free choice, transcendental freedom is manifested, realized, and actualized precisely in freedom of choice. Our fundamental response to God is realized in these everyday concrete choices. Just as God's presence is mediated to us so, too, our response to God is mediated in our individual choices. These individual choices manifest our deepest orientation just as a tree's fruit bears witness to the tree's health. These individual choices, acts of categorical freedom, in turn influence the strength and direction of our orientation, either reinforcing the fundamental option or weakening it.

The task of the Christian life, therefore, is to orient one's life toward God and, over a lifetime, to dispose oneself more fully toward God so that one may come to love God with one's whole heart, soul, mind, and strength. This development of the positive fundamental option is clearly both a spiritual and a moral task. The reinforcement of one's orientation toward God is clearly a function of prayer, but just as much is it a task of aligning one's individual choices with the basic direction of one's orientation.

The fundamental disposing of one's life for God, then, requires the difficult and lifelong effort of integrating all of one's choices and attitudes into this fundamental choice for God. This requires an active effort to develop the virtues—habitual dispositions to choose the good. As the integration of self progresses, the positive fundamental option cannot be easily reversed but moves by the ongoing cooperation of human effort with grace to a complete and total response to God. The development and growth of the positive fundamental option, therefore, requires both prayer and growth in virtue. The insights of the Three Ways are thus already anticipated here in the unity of our spiritual and moral striving.

Fundamental option theories of sin have been criticized from a number of different perspectives.[5] This is not the place to enter into a prolonged discussion of these critiques, but one major line of criticism in particular should be noted. Some critics argue that the distinction between transcendental and categorical freedom—and thus the discussion of a level of freedom not fully available to reflexive consciousness—results in a form of dualism in which the person as subject is separated from his or her acts. As the discussion below will indicate, it is a longstanding tenet of the Christian spiritual life that God works most profoundly at a level "too deep for words"—deep within the person's heart where the person is truly touched by God although his or her conscious experience may be one of profound aridity. In light of the fundamental option theory, the "heart" is precisely this deep and always somewhat hidden core in which the person disposes self to God.

The Three Ways

The Christian spiritual tradition has long understood the spiritual life to develop in dynamic fashion through certain identifiable stages[6]—sometimes divided into two stages (active and contemplative; *praktikos* and *gnosis*), more often since the Middle Ages, into three stages. This three-stage spiritual development came to be known as the Three Ways—beginners, proficients, and the perfect—or the purgative, illuminative, and unitive ways. These two sets of terms have become virtually interchangeable.

The point of identifying the Three Ways in the Christian life is not to suggest a linear development through discrete and logical steps, as if one successfully and finally completes one stage and then moves on to the next. Purgation or purification, for example, occurs not only early in spiritual development but characterizes the later stages, though at a deeper level. Rather, the Three Ways point to the basic dynamism of the Christian life—the life of ongoing or continual conversion. The struggles of the Christian life are an effort—always with the help of grace—to surrender more fully to God and to the demands of Christian living. As the Christian progresses, the spiritual life is marked by a greater simplicity in prayer and in life as the person experiences a greater inner unity and deeper integration.

Before looking briefly at each stage of the Three Ways it must be noted immediately that the first two ways, of purgation and illumination, are notably moral. They presuppose that any growth in prayer and in holiness requires a moral conversion and vice versa. For the person to grow in holiness he or she must grow as a person of virtue. To become holy, one must become truly good. It is no accident that traditional ascetical-mystical manuals devoted no less attention to virtue than did the traditional manuals of moral theology; in fact, the ascetical-mystical manuals devoted far *more* attention to growth in virtue, since the moral manuals were often focused on the moral analysis of individual human *acts*.

The necessary connection between spiritual and moral growth as envisioned in the Three Ways is consistent with the relationship between religious and moral conversion discussed in the previous chapter. Religious conversion flows out into moral conversion since the "splendor" of values is revealed in a new way to one whose vision has been transformed by the "other-worldly falling in love" of religious conversion. To choose values over mere satisfactions constitutes moral conversion, and the ability to choose values consistently is precisely the life of virtue. At the same time, the self-transcendence realized in moral conversion points at least potentially and implicitly to the total self-transcendence to which religious conversion directs the person. The Three Ways, then, represents a traditional way of under-standing and directing ongoing conversion.

The Purgative Way

The purgative way, or the way of beginners, is marked by the progressive purgation or purification of the senses from the attachments which hinder the person from surrendering self totally to God. Purgation aims at a greater inner freedom to respond to God's self-offer. The purgative way thus presupposes an initial awakening to God's presence and call as well as an awareness of the various attachments which keep one from responding to God freely and totally.

Prayer in the purgative way, being in its initial stages, is largely discursive and involves the use of prayers composed by others and by explicitly verbal, if silent, "talking" to God. The beginner, with the help of grace, devotes a great deal of attention to the avoidance of the sin which characterized his or her past life. This detachment from sin and its enticements involves atonement and contrition for past sin as a detachment from its continuing power. It involves, as well, an active mortification through the deliberate choice of what is difficult and disagree-able in an effort to reverse habitual patterns of attachment.

The way of purgation, then, is necessarily a struggle; it is a slow and painful confrontation with one's bad habits (vices), with sinful concupiscence, and with what we might call today the "sin of the world." The process of detachment is a painful one; but, as beginners grow in prayer and in discipline, they can be encouraged by their ability to see more clearly the hindrances created by their various attachments and by the success of their initial efforts to become free of these attachments. Any new clarity of vision or success is, of course, to be attributed to the action of God's grace with which the Christian strives increasingly to cooperate.

In more contemporary terms we might call the purgative way the effort to integrate all of our desires and choices into our fundamental desire and orientation for God. It is the effort to release our freedom from the bondage to those things that cannot fulfill our deepest longings. Only in overcoming this bondage can we be truly free to love God and other persons. This purgation must be characteristic of all of the stages of spiritual growth as the person seeks to reverse the disordered orientation and attachments of sin. Turning from the illusion of finding security and ultimate meaning in created goods, the Christian commits himself or herself to turn to God and to conform every aspect of his or her life to a fundamental response to God.

As we have seen, the lifelong effort at integration (purgation, purification) is a painful process of transcending all that is false. It is, therefore, a share in the cross, a dying with Christ. In the monastic tradition of John Cassian and St. Benedict, it is the way of humility leading to purity of heart; in the Carmelite tradition, the total surrender of self; for Thomas Merton, the putting to death of the false self so that the true and deepest self may truly live; or what we might call an ongoing self-transcendence in love. We can see, therefore, how the purgative way is the early stage in the ongoing development of a positive fundamental option, the integration of one's choices into one's fundamental orientation toward God.

The Illuminative Way

The illuminative way, or the way of proficients, is characterized by a deepening of prayer—a move from discursive to a more affective prayer. Prayer becomes more personal—"from the heart"—and eventually less wordy. One's prayer is, in a sense, further "illuminated" by a greater openness to the divine light. At the same time, there is the ongoing effort to grow in virtue, the persistent endeavor at integration at deeper levels. As the proficient grows closer to God, he or she develops an increasing awareness of the roots of one's sin, and thus the attack on sin moves beyond merely avoiding individual sinful acts to a more concerted effort to root out sinful habits and attitudes. We see here the further and deeper integration of choice and attitude in the developing positive fundamental option.

But the way of proficients is not "illuminative" only because of an increased illumination in prayer, or a gradual movement away from the darkness of sin, but because of the illumination that comes with the growth of charity. As one becomes increasingly free of attachments, of self, one is more free to love. As the person's life is more conformed to the Love to which he or she is drawing near, the person more clearly manifests the image of God who is love. One begins to see with the eyes of love so that love begins to illuminate all that one surveys and empowers one to do the good. (In the previous chapter we discussed the way in which affective conversion—the modality of self-transcendence that becomes possible when the person is transformed by love— empowers moral conversion.) Charity, therefore, comes to inform all of the virtues and thus all of the person's actions. Love comes so to conform the proficient's will to God's loving will that St. Augustine's dictum can become a lived reality: "Love and do what you will."

We see, therefore, in the illuminative way, an increasing unity within the proficient of the love of God and love of neighbor. There is a further integration of the love of God which has become the focus of one's spiritual life, and the love of neighbor which has been the focus of one's moral striving. The love of God becomes more manifestly mediated in love of neighbor and vice versa.[7] It is in this light that we can understand the judgment scene of Matthew 25 in which men and women are judged by their attention to their least brothers and sisters, and the Johannine identification of love of God and love of brothers and sisters (1 Jn 4:20–21).

Although the proficient's prayer has grown and deepened, he or she will still experience periods of dryness in prayer. These periods should not be allowed to lead to a spirit of discouragement, for the person should trust that God continues to work at a level "beneath" the person's conscious awareness. Similarly, while the proficient will experience periods of consolation and feelings of God's presence, the proficient may enjoy but should not cling to such feelings. They may be genuine mediations or fruits of God's presence, but they may also be self-deceptions. To cling even to genuine consolations is to make of them further attachments which only hinder further growth and integration.

The Dark Night

The passage from the illuminative to the unitive way, from proficient to perfect, is marked by a particularly intense period of darkness and aridity, described classically by St. John of the Cross as the dark night of the soul. No longer is God experienced in affective prayer; the person feels abandoned, bereft of God. And yet, what distinguishes the dark night from a commonplace period of dryness in prayer or the result of one's own dissipation is the ongoing *desire* to pray that indicates the continuing longing, orientation, of the soul toward God.

Although the person *experiences* only darkness, in fact the person has drawn closer to God—so close that God can no longer be known in the categories of ordinary experience and intellect. Their mediation of the divine presence and of an authentic knowledge of God is revealed to be "as so much chaff" as St. Thomas Aquinas is reported to have said of his own monumental theological work as his holy life drew to a close. The light of God's presence has drawn so close that the person is blinded and experiences the light as darkness. God is at work, present, at a level so deep that the person can have no conscious awareness of it, no experience, no reflexive knowledge. At the point of the dark night, the task of integrating all of one's desires into one's most basic desire for God has reached the point that one's self-disposal is on the verge of a final and total surrender to the living God— the surrender even of attachments to one's cherished experiences, images, and concepts of God.

Paradoxically perhaps, it is the experience of the dark night of the soul that best illuminates the presence of a fundamental option. The person experiences this period as darkness, not only because of the closeness of God's sublime light but also because the soul is touched at a level too deep for consciousness or reflexive knowledge. That such a transcendental level exists seems to be a presupposition of the Christian mystical tradition. It is trust in God's action at this level that enables the person to remain faithful through the ordinary periods of aridity in prayer and especially through the experience of the dark night. That God is present at a level and in a way too deep for ordinary conscious experience was a presupposition of the advice of mystical authors not to trust or cling to consolations and mere *feelings* of God's presence (or absence).

In a sense, after a long period of integration, the deepening of the spiritual life has become focused at the deepest core of the person, at the level of the transcendental. This is the deepest personal core which Häring, following biblical authors, calls the "heart"; which Merton calls the "true self"; or which we may call the "fundamental option." It is the truest level of the person in which the disciple's life is "hidden with Christ in God" (Col 3:3). To say, then, that one's fundamental option occurs at a level too deep for reflexive consciousness is merely to point to the deepest core of the person where, according to our spiritual tradition, Heart speaks to heart, where the human heart says its profoundest "yes" to God. At the threshold between the illuminative and the unitive, the fundamental option is at the verge of a definitive "yes"; the total self-surrender of other-worldly falling in love is on the verge of being complete.

The Unitive Way

At last, in the unitive way, the person has transcended the moral life. Or, perhaps it is more accurate to use Lonergan's term "sublation." The moral life has been "sublated" into the transcendent—that is, it is not repudiated or destroyed but carried into a higher level, realized in a richer context. As the integration of self in the development of the positive funda-mental option progresses, reversals and contradictions become less possible. As the author of *The Cloud of Unknowing* (ch. 48) states, the mystics come to know good and evil by intuition. Finally, in the unitive way, the person has attained such an integral orientation toward God that any actions which are contrary to this fundamental option become a virtual impossibility.

The sublation of the moral life in the unitive way is manifest in the flowering of the gifts of the Holy Spirit. As the purgative way is characterized by the elimination of vice, and the illuminative way by growth in virtue, the unitive way is characterized by the predominance of the gifts. Traditionally identified as wisdom, understanding, knowledge, counsel, piety, fortitude and fear of the Lord, these seven gifts are stable dispositions of openness to divine promptings. In a sense, the gifts perfect the virtues by directing them, now more perfectly aligned with charity, to God. The human will, conformed to the divine will by long effort, needs only the slightest promptings of the Spirit in order to respond. The virtues and prayers of the proficient have created a heart open and docile to the action of the Spirit, a docility which is the necessary ground for the gift of contemplation. The person, increasingly single-hearted in his or her orientation and attention to the divine, is more sensitive to the Beloved's presence, whisperings, urgings.

In the unitive way, the perfect have come to the penultimate fulfillment of all their striving, moral and spiritual. Lives which have been dedicated to orienting all desire to God, integrating all choices into the fundamental "choice" for God, reach a state of union with God, a simple resting in the divine life on earth. Here mystical authors speak of "spiritual marriage" between the soul and God. The person's fundamental orientation has brought the person at last to the closest union with God attainable in this life—which is still a mere foretaste of the life to come.

Conclusion

God has created every human heart with a capacity for the infinite, a longing desire for communion which God alone can satisfy. In Jesus, God has spoken the definitive word of self-offering; in Jesus, God has given the model for the human response; and in Jesus and through the work of the Holy Spirit, God has made an authentic human response possible. What response can human creatures make to the infinite God who calls sinful men and women into communion except one that is total and complete? What response except one that includes all desire, all choice, every aspect of the creature's life? In short, to love the God who has first loved us with all our heart, soul, mind, and strength.

Tragically, in a world laden with sin, in a personal existence tainted by original sin and burdened by vices and the effects of sin, this total response of the human person requires a lifetime of effort—always initiated, supported, corrected, and perfected by grace. This graced effort to overcome the attachment and bondage of sin so that the person can respond to God with all of his or her being is the integrating effort of the fundamental option, the life of ongoing conversion. It is this foundational "yes" to God—weak and tentative at first—which leads the person to struggle through purgation and illumination to attain the union for which the person was created, to which he or she is called, and except for which he or she cannot be wholly satisfied.

It is, then, the person's fundamental option, rooted in the experience of conversion, that drives the person—with the promptings of grace—through all the struggles of detachment, the overcoming of vice, the growth in virtue, the patient and trusting endurance of trial and aridity. It is the fundamental option which is the dynamic principle of the Christian life in which the person seeks to make total and definitive his or her "yes" to God's gracious self-offering. The Three Ways are, finally, different levels of this single way of one's fundamental life orientation toward God. The moral life and the spiritual life are two intimately interrelated aspects of the life which seeks to surrender *all* to God. As one draws closer to God, the seemingly disparate aspects of one's strivings become more clearly one— like the streams and brooks and creeks which feed a single river that empties finally into the sea, vast and wide. The individual self remains, but the person is one with the triune God.

4

GOAL AND PRESENT REALITY: PARTICIPATION IN DIVINE LIFE

The author of the second letter of Peter holds out to Christians the hope of becoming "sharers in the divine nature" (1:4). Drawing on this and other biblical passages, a number of Greek and Latin patristic authors affirmed that "God became human in order that humans might become divine." In this perspective, sharing or participation in the divine life—becoming God by participation—is the very goal and purpose of the Christian life. Especially in the Eastern Christian tradition, *theosis* or *theopoiesis* (becoming God, deification, divinization) has been understood to describe the sweep of Christian existence from creation in God's image to final union with God. Therefore, to reflect at all on Christian faith and life, on Christian moral living and prayer, requires attention to the goal and reality of *theosis*. It is in this context of viewing each Christian's life as directed toward and given meaning by *theosis* that Orthodox and Eastern Catholic theology has understood the unity of the moral and spiritual life as well as the inseparability of dogmatic, moral and spiritual theology.

It is the purpose of this chapter to suggest that retrieving the concept of *theosis* as a way of understanding the meaning and goal of Christian living may offer some important suggestions for Roman Catholic moral theology and spirituality. *Theosis* serves in

Orthodox theology to specify both the goal of the Christian life as well as the authentic shape of present striving.

Retrieval of a greater emphasis on *theosis* in Western theology can serve a similar function—specifying both the goal of ongoing conversion and the authentic shape of the integrating work of the Christian's fundamental option. Thus, the understanding of sharing in the divine life itself may help to attain a greater appreciation of the unity of moral and spiritual striving in the life of every Christian.

The chapter begins with a brief summary of the synthesis of moral and spiritual theology as understood by Thomas Aquinas, focusing on attaining the ultimate end as the unifying principle of Christian life. The Orthodox understanding of *theosis* as the meaning and goal of Christian striving will be examined in some greater detail, followed by some critical comments from a Roman Catholic perspective. The chapter will conclude with some suggestions concerning the value of retrieving the concept of *theosis* for a more complete under-standing of Roman Catholic moral theology and spirituality.

The Thomistic Synthesis of Ethics and Spirituality

For Thomas Aquinas, the whole of the Christian's life was directed to the attainment of the ultimate end, the beatific vision or union with God. In the context of this goal, one could understand the moral and spiritual life of every Christian. Through human effort, aided by grace, each Christian worked to overcome sin and grew in acquired virtue. This moral preparation further disposed one to deeper prayer. Meanwhile, the ongoing life of prayer and the grace made available in the sacraments infused the Christian with new virtues and directed his or her actions and dispositions toward the ultimate end, toward God. In this perspective, there may be a notional distinction drawn between the moral life and the spiritual life of Christians, but no true separation can be made between them.

The Second Part of the *Summa Theologiae*, which deals with the moral life, begins with a discussion of the ultimate end, placing moral theology into a secure context in the journey of faith. As our earlier historical overview in chapter 1 has shown, the greater specialization of theology after Aquinas and the development of moral theology as a separate discipline led eventually, however, to separating moral theology from its theological roots. A text on moral theology published by John Azor (d. 1603) dropped the opening treatise on beatitude, the ultimate end;[1] and in the ages that followed, discussion of the ultimate end and its relationship to the moral life of the individual Christian became more remote. Many of the nineteenth and twentieth century manuals of moral theology began formally with a brief discussion of beatitude as the ultimate end, maintaining a formal relationship with the synthesis of Aquinas. But these works then proceeded to discuss the moral life as if it were virtually unrelated to the ultimate end.[2] Moral theology became focused on acts, laws, minimums, and avoiding sin with very little attention to growth in virtue enabled by prayer and to deepening prayer sustained by a developing moral goodness. Moral theology became the discipline for guiding the ordinary lay person, while spiritual theology became the discipline for the elite few called to true holiness. Thus, the ordinary person could aspire to become good, and an elite few could strive to become truly holy. By no means contrary to these goals, but at least apparently more sublime, is the aspiration held out to Eastern Christians to become not only good and holy but to become sharers in the divine.

Theosis in Orthodox Thought

Theosis is a common theme of Orthodox spiritual theology[3] and Orthodox ethics[4] as these disciplines have developed in recent times into relatively distinct—though not separate— areas of study. The concept is rooted in certain key passages in the New Testament, but developed especially by certain Greek Fathers and later theologians such as Athanasius, the Cappadocian Fathers, Maximus Confessor, Gregory Palamas, and Nicolas Cabasilas.[5] The concept is not foreign to Western Christianity, grounded as it is in common patristic sources, but the concept of *theosis* has not been developed so consistently nor as a central focus for an understanding of Christian life.[6] It is not within the scope of the present study to develop the history of the concept of *theosis* nor to compare its development in East and West. It is important here to examine how the concept of *theosis* and certain related concepts function together in Orthodox thought in bringing the moral and spiritual life of the Christian into a coherent whole. Of course, even this more limited purpose cannot hope to capture the breadth or the depth of this central concept of the Eastern Christian spiritual and moral tradition.

The Orthodox concept of *theosis*, as a growing participation of human persons in the divine life, flows from a particular emphasis on the triune God in relationship with humankind. In fact, Orthodox trinitarian theology of God has tended to focus greater attention on the external relationship of the Persons of the Trinity to humanity as opposed to the relatively greater attention in the West on the *inner* life of the Trinity.[7]

Orthodox reflection on the triune God, then, is the foundation of its reflection on *theosis*; and the fact that God is triune comes to be an important foundation for understanding both the divine action in deification as well as human persons themselves, since humanity is created in the image of the *triune* God.

It is precisely because human persons are created in the image of God that they are destined to participate in the divine life, that is, to be deified.[8] *Theosis* is nothing other than the full and final realization of the creation of the human person in God's image. In fact, for human persons to be fully and authentically human, they must grow in similitude to God in whose image they were created.[9] Many Orthodox theologians highlight the further distinction pursued by some patristic sources (in Greek more than Latin sources) between image and likeness, since the Genesis text (Gen 1:26) uses both terms. After the fall, the image of God in the human person remains, although it is now tarnished, making the realization of likeness to God more difficult to attain.

Theosis, then, involves a purifying of the image of God with the goal of realizing the likeness to God. Image represents human nature as given, while likeness represents the dynamism of realizing the image. Likeness comes to represent a goal of Christian striving.[10] This central focus of theological anthropology on the human person as image of God becomes the foundation of Christian ethics since it is the task of ethics to guide the Christian in the restoration and perfection of God's image that has been tarnished by sin. As Orthodox ethicist Stanley Harakas suggests, the "doctrine of the image" is the "linchpin of Orthodox ethics."[11]

But to speak of *theosis* as a full realization of creation in God's image is not meant to suggest a natural progression nor a flowering of human nature by human effort. Ultimately *theosis* is God's gift and becomes an actual possibility only because of the work of the Son and the Holy Spirit. It is in taking on human nature in the incarnation that the Son of God makes *theosis* possible for men and women.[12] Christ's salvific or redemptive work— so much the emphasis of Western theology—is understood to be one aspect of this broader divine purpose of deification:

> Considered from the point of view of our fallen state, the aim of the divine dispensation can be termed salvation or redemption. This is the negative aspect of our ultimate goal, which is considered from the perspective of our sin. Considered from the point of view of the ultimate vocation of created beings, the aim of the divine dispensation can be termed deification. This is the positive definition of the same mystery....[13]

The transfiguration of Jesus, recorded in the gospels, serves as a foretaste and promise of the transfiguration of a deified humanity in Christ.[14] Realizing the image of God through *theosis* becomes a realizing of the image of Christ, both divine and human, who is the archetype of God's image and its perfect realization. Deification, then, becomes a process of "Christification."[15] This Christification does involve a certain growth through imitation and following of Christ, but even more it involves an actual participation in Christ's life through the action of the Holy Spirit in the life of the church.

The deification of humanity is not a "work" of any one of the divine Persons but of the entire Trinity. Orthodox theologian

George Mantzaridis summarizes: "The orientation of man toward the Father and his deification is the common accomplishment of the Trinity, brought about through the love of the Father by the Son in the Holy Spirit."[16] Thus, while the concept of *theosis* is rooted in the trinitarian understanding of God, it is at the same time grounded in Christology and pneumatology: "The Son has become like us by the incarnation; we become like him by deification, by partaking of the divinity in the Holy Spirit, who communicates the divinity to each human person in a particular way."[17]

The process of theosis in the life of the Christian is both a spiritual and a moral task, one that involves the whole person. As Harakas maintains, the Christian must try to realize a *politeia* of *theosis*, that is, deification as an entire and holistic way of life. The way of life can be called "growth in Christ" or "living in the Spirit" or "living sacramentally," but all of these refer to a fundamental reorientation or transformation of one's whole life empowered by grace.[18] The way of *theosis* necessarily involves moral struggle *(askesis)* in the effort to overcome sin and to grow in the virtues that manifest that Christians are living even now the attributes of God whose image in themselves they are striving to restore. But inseparable from this essentially moral struggle is the spiritual struggle to grow in prayer in which Christians encounter the God by whose power alone human life can be deified. As Vladimir Lossky says of growth in virtue, love, and prayer:

> All the virtues together subserve perfection in prayer; while the virtues cannot possibly be assured if the Spirit is not constantly turned toward prayer. Moreover, the greatest of the virtues, charity, that love of God in which the mystical union is accomplished is itself the fruit of prayer....[19]

The Christian way of life and *theosis* itself, then, as patristic authors analyzed it, consist in both the purification of the "active" life *(praxis)* and the deep communion with God of the "contemplative" life *(theoria)*.[20] Vigen Guroian summarizes the interrelationship of moral and spiritual striving: "The moral life in all of its conscientious attention and striving for the good is finally taken up into the spiritual life. For the good is not simply the norm of life; it is the divine life itself."[21]

Participation in the divine life—both as the ultimate goal and as proleptically present—impacts the moral life of the Christian in a number of ways. In moral decisions and actions, Christians must strive to act in such a way as to bring them closer to their goal of *theosis*. Deification, then, functions in a way similar to the functioning of the ultimate end in a Thomistic, teleological moral theology. The striving to attain the good (and ultimately the Good which is God) does not justify any means, of course, but it is this striving for the good (and for the Good) which is the very purpose for any authentic human action and which is the most basic criterion for determining moral goodness.[22] At the same time though, *theosis* as goal and as present reality enlightens the Christian moral life more broadly. The process of *theosis* requires developing those attitudes, dispositions, virtues, and character that are appropriate to one created in the image of God and moving toward *theosis*. These attributes are modelled in the first instance by God in the divine interaction with humanity, by Christ, and by the saints celebrated in the liturgical cycle.[23] This, too, does not seem dissimilar to the type of "virtue teleology" that characterizes the moral theology of Aquinas— with all of his emphasis on the development of virtues ultimately to be formed by love for the attainment of communion with God. The goal of *theosis*, then, impacts the Christian moral life both at the level of decisions and at the level of character—what contemporary Christian ethics refers to as the "ethics of doing" and the "ethics of being."[24]

To speak of *theosis* as a task is not to deny that ultimately it is a gift. It is accomplished by "synergy" between the divine and human wills, a cooperation of human effort with divine initiative and free gift. Grace is seen to be utterly essential to the process of deification—grace understood as the working of the "divine energies" with the human will. While from the human perspective, the struggle may seem largely the result of human effort, in fact, from the divine perspective the same process is ultimately the result of divine action.[25]

Further, though *theosis* is the goal and task of every

Christian life and a gift given by God to the individual, it is by no means only individual or private. The human person is inherently relational—in relationship with other human persons. This reality flows from the creation of humanity in the image of the triune God. Just as the triune God is three Persons in one nature, so all men and women are individual human persons sharing a single nature.[26] It is precisely this common human nature that has been taken on by the Son of God and deified in him in anticipation of the deification of humankind. Furthermore, the realization of the reign of God proclaimed by and manifest in Jesus further requires a communitarian understanding of the Christian life and of Christian ethics and spirituality. The Christian life, then, and the process of *theosis* are ultimately and necessarily relational and communitarian. This is the foundation of Orthodox social ethics[27]—and the reason that all authentically Christian ethics and spirituality are social as well as personal.

The church itself is a "communion of deification."[28] In baptism, its members are joined to Christ and initiated on the path of *theosis*; in chrismation/confirmation, they are sealed by the Holy Spirit for this task; in the eucharist, they are nourished by the encounter with Christ who is the source and hope of deified life. The church, then, and the life of each Christian on the path of *theosis* are centered in the life of worship and sacrament, most especially in the eucharist. The life of Christians—their moral and spiritual striving for participation in the divine life—must always be rooted in the liturgy; and both Christian ethics and spirituality must be fundamentally grounded in the church's celebration of the sacred liturgy.[29]

Critique

As has been noted above, the concept of *theosis* has not occupied the central place in Western theology that it has occupied in the East.[30] It certainly has not become a unifying principle for theology, ethics and spirituality as it has in the Eastern Christian tradition. It is interesting to note, however, that deification continued to occupy an important place in

Western mystical writings—a mystical "intuition," perhaps, of its importance for the Christian spiritual life.[31] In any case, reference to deification is virtually absent from the major Roman Catholic ascetical and mystical manuals of this century.[32] Being absent from such manuals, *theosis* could not regain a central place in Roman Catholic spiritual theology and in the lived spirituality of those who learned from them.

The different emphases of Western theology in general, and of contemporary Roman Catholic theological discussion in particular, would suggest a number of critical remarks about any attempt to retrieve the concept of *theosis* into Catholic moral theology and spirituality. At least four of these areas of possible criticism from the perspective of Roman Catholic ethics and spirituality must be addressed: First, it could be argued that the concept is not biblical in contrast to the concerted efforts of contemporary moral theology and spirituality to return to their biblical roots. Second, it can be argued that the concept of *theosis* as developed in Orthodox spirituality and ethics presupposes a "Christology from above" that is at odds with a more contemporary Roman Catholic emphasis on a "Christology from below" rooted in biblical testimony. Third, it might be argued that the concept of *theosis* and the theology that grounds it does not sufficiently address the structural dimensions of social existence and thus that it does not adequately direct the Christian to the struggle for the kingdom in the contemporary economic and political order. Finally, it could be argued that the goal of *theosis* as an organizing principle for the moral and spiritual life is precisely teleological when many contemporary Roman Catholic moral theologians are arguing for a model of the moral life which is neither teleological nor deontological. It is apparent that critiques such as these must be addressed, at least briefly, before suggesting how the concept of *theosis* can be enlightening for Catholic moral theology and spirituality.

While a number of biblical passages (e.g., Jn 17:21; Rom 2:7; 1 Cor 15:52; Eph 1:10; 2 Tim 1:10) may *suggest* some aspect of *theosis*, it is really only one verse in the relatively late second letter of Peter (1:4) that refers explicitly to becoming "sharers in the divine nature." This has suggested to some that the concept is more the fruit of Neoplatonic thought and of general Hellenistic religiosity than an idea rooted in biblical sources.[33] Orthodox theologians, without denying the Hellenistic influence, have attempted to lay out the broader biblical basis for the concept.[34] Furthermore, it must be acknowledged that the Christian understanding of incorporation into Christ through the working of the Holy Spirit, together with trinitarian doctrine itself, developed only in the ongoing reflection of the post-apostolic church. The concept of *theosis*, dependent on this trinitarian foundation, could not have developed in mature form until after the apostolic period. In their reflection on the Trinity, the Greek Fathers "sought to clarify how God's relationship to us in Christ and the Spirit in the economy of the Incarnation and deification reveals the essential unity and equality of Father, Son, and Spirit."[35] It may be precisely the contemporary renewal of trinitarian studies in the West, with a greater emphasis on the relationship of the Trinity with humankind, that can suggest the value of the concept of *theosis* for understanding the Christian moral and spiritual life in the context of the individual Christian's relationship with the triune God.[36]

The Orthodox insistence that each Christian touches the "divine energies" rather than the divine nature itself attempts to preserve Orthodoxy's insistence on the transcendence of God.[37] Further, the very trinitarian starting point for the concept of deification suggests a "Christology from above," one that emphasizes the preexistent second Person of the Trinity not to the exclusion but to the relative de-emphasis on the human Jesus. The Orthodox emphasis on the divine transcendence and a "Christology from above" is by no means foreign to Western theology.[38] Still, it seems to run contrary to a greater contemporary emphasis in the West on the immanence of God and the humanity of Jesus.

It might be argued, then, that the concept of *theosis* cannot be reconciled with current trends in Catholic theology. This need not be the case. The Orthodox emphasis on the relationship of the triune God to humanity has always held together the affirmation both of divine transcendence and of divine immanence. This same emphasis is receiving renewed attention in Roman Catholic trinitarian theology, as Catherine LaCugna's recent work on the Trinity, significantly entitled *God for Us*, manifests.[39] Furthermore, although the Western emphasis on "Christologies from below" has been understood to offer a useful corrective to an almost exclusive emphasis on "Christologies from above," many contemporary Christologists are attempting to draw together the insights of both types into a more adequate whole.[40]

The insights of Orthodox theologian Panayiotis Nellas into deification as Christification suggests the Christocentrism of the concept of *theosis*. The incarnation of the preexistent Son of God makes *theosis* possible for those creatures whose nature he has deified by taking it upon himself. His life, death, and resurrection manifest the way of deification; and it is participation in his risen life through the Holy Spirit in the life of the church that anticipates and enables the process of *theosis* in the actual life of Christians. In daily Christian living, then, it is precisely the path of discipleship—following Jesus through the cross and sharing in his life through the sacraments of the church—that is the path of *theosis*.[41] A life focused on the life, death, and resurrection of Jesus—so much the emphasis of contemporary Roman Catholic ethics and spirituality—can itself be understood as the authentic path of *theosis*.

In briefly examining the use of trinitarian theology in Orthodox ethics and its doctrine of *theosis*, Catherine LaCugna suggests that it does not adequately address the social and structural implications of the Christian message.[42] LaCugna, together with the emphases of liberation theologies, places greater emphasis on the social ramifications of the theology of the Trinity.[43] Whether LaCugna's reading of contemporary Orthodox ethics is entirely accurate or not, the Orthodox doctrine of *theosis* need not be individualistic, as she herself implies.[44] As has been noted above, the creation of humanity in the image of the triune God grounds a relational understanding of the human person— perhaps better, it might be said, than a Western anthropology that usually begins with a philosophical focus on the freedom and self-determination of the individual and only later attends to the person as relational or social. The trinitarian focus of Orthodox anthropology itself implies the necessity of establishing right relationships and authentic communion in every aspect of human life and interaction in order authentically to image the life of the Trinity. A similar anthropological starting point might well serve Western Christian ethics and spirituality in attending to the structural dimensions of human existence.

Some contemporary Roman Catholic ethicists have argued that a teleological model of the moral life—such as the traditional Thomistic understanding of the moral life aimed at the ultimate end—is no longer the best or most authentic model for Christian self-understanding.[45] To the degree that *theosis* functions as a goal of the Christian moral life, it would seem to be included in this critique. Roman Catholic moral theologians Bernard Häring and Charles Curran, together with Protestant ethicists H. Richard Niebuhr and James Gustafson, have argued for a "relationality-responsibility" model that does not understand the moral life and moral decision-making so much as aimed at a goal, but as the authentic response of the Christian to what God is "enabling and requiring" at the present moment. Christians do not so much seek to conform their lives to a remote goal but rather to live responsibly and to respond authentically to the God who has invited them into relationship.

The concept of *theosis* does suggest a teleological understanding of the moral life inasmuch as deification remains a goal or end of the Christian life. At the same time, however, *theosis* does not describe merely a remote goal but a developing present reality. Creation in God's image, the incarnation, and the working of the Holy Spirit in the life of the church make the Christian already a participant in the divine life. The demands of *theosis*, then, are the current demands of one living in relationship with God—realizing the image of God in oneself and responding to the working of the Holy Spirit in one's daily existence. The concept of *theosis*, then, can allow both for an appreciation of union with God as the ultimate goal or end of Christian life as well as for an affirmation that it is precisely through present relationship and response to God that this end is already manifest and finally attained.

Living the Life of Theosis

The purpose of this brief study of the concept of *theosis* as it is developed in Orthodox theology has been to suggest its value for Roman Catholic ethics and spirituality—and in particular for providing a broader context in which the unity of ethics and spirituality could be more evident. To understand the Christian life as a path of *theosis* is to suggest that the human person is called not "merely" into relationship with God—as truly incredible as that is in itself—but that human persons are invited and called into a share in the divine life itself, into the very inner life of the triune God. This participation in God's life is a future goal, but it is also a present reality because of each Christian's incorporation into Christ and the work of the Holy Spirit in the life of the church. The Christian life—moral and spiritual—is the graced effort to celebrate the gift, to manifest the reality authentically, and to realize the goal of becoming divine by participation.

Because *theosis* is ultimately a gift from God, the foundational Christian affection must be gratitude. As Bernard Häring has long argued, the Christian's grateful response takes two basic forms: worship (communal and personal) and moral living (being and doing).[16] In worship, Christians celebrate the gift offered by God—in the personal worship of prayer and in the communal worship of the liturgy, most especially the eucharist. All authentic Christian spirituality must flow from this grateful response to God's free offering, and thus all authentic Christian spirituality is rooted in the church's celebration of the liturgy.

Distinct from but intertwined with the individual Christian's response to God in worship is the response of moral living. The Christian strives to act as and to become the kind of person that is an authentic response and reflection of the divine gift—the gift of participation in the inner life and love of the Trinity. In seeking an authentic response, the Christian looks to Jesus Christ, divine and human, who is the most perfect manifestation of the gift and of the response to the divine gift. The Christian moral life, then, is not in the first instance about duty and law but about *gratitude and the loving response* to love and life offered. Christian spirituality and ethics, then, are ultimately rooted and remain united in the grateful response of Christians to God's offer of deified life in Christ through the action of the Holy Spirit.

Because *theosis* is a present reality—though only partially realized—Christians strive to live a life in conformity to the awesome dignity to which they are called. In grace, the Trinity already dwells in the heart of every Christian, an indwelling that is plumbed more deeply as the Christian enters more intensely into the hidden silence of contemplative prayer. Christian spirituality, then, is rooted in the belief that the Trinity already dwells within, and that we already share in the divine life through grace, in prayer, both personal and communal.

To believe that one already shares in the divine life demands of the Christian an authentic response to the divine life and love, most especially as this has been revealed in Jesus Christ. Christians strive to model in their lives those perspectives, dispositions, virtues, attitudes, intentions, and affections that seem authentic to the deified life which they have already begun to live, although as yet incompletely and imperfectly. Believers strive to decide and to act in a way consistent with their new life and with the character which flows from it. Christian ethics—both of doing and of being—must be profoundly rooted in the reality of *theosis*.

Because *theosis* remains ever a goal in present existence, the moral and spiritual life of the Christian is always characterized by a striving, a struggle, a dynamism. Here the traditions of both the East and the West are united in seeing the progression of the Christian life as inescapably moral and spiritual, overcoming sin and growing in virtue empowered by a developing life of prayer and an increasing depth and richness of prayer founded on the fertile ground of a virtuous life. Whether one speaks of the active and contemplative life *(praxis* and *theoria)* or of the Three Ways of purgation, illumination, and union, the Christian tradition has upheld the unity of moral and spiritual striving. *Theosis*, though ultimately gift, is prepared for by the cooperation of human effort in moral and spiritual growth.

Contemporary Roman Catholic ethics and spirituality have both been challenged to overcome the individualism that has characterized their recent forms and to develop instead a keen recognition of the social nature of humanity and of the goal of human striving. Furthermore, both have been challenged to incorporate the Christian's duty to seek justice and liberation in the contemporary historical order as essential to any authentic Christian life. *Theosis*—grounded in the creation of humankind in the image of a triune and relational God and directed to the common life in the inner life of the three-Personed God— can provide the theological and anthropological basis for this social perspective. Those created in the image of the Trinity and who hope to participate in the inner life of the triune God are relational, and they must seek authentic relationship and communion with others in order to attain an authentic humanity. (The pursuit of authentic relationships is the topic of the next chapter.) Just and loving relationships—both interpersonal and structural—are essential to those who are on the path of *theosis*. The church itself, as the community of deification, must witness in itself the authenticity of relationships and must call the world to the same authentic humanity. The celebration of the church's liturgy celebrates new relationships with God and others in Christ, and it challenges the church to pursue such relationships in the world.

And, finally, the fact that deification is ultimately Christification points to the necessary Christocentrism of both Christian ethics and Christian spirituality. It is Christ, the incarnate Son of God, who deifies human nature in himself and who makes *theosis* a possibility for his brothers and sisters through his death and resurrection. It is Christ who is the perfect image of God and the perfect realization of deified humanity. It is by conformity to Christ through baptism, chrismation/confirmation, and eucharist, through participation in his risen life through the Holy Spirit in the life of the church, and through a life of faithful discipleship leading through the cross that Christians follow Christ into the divine life which is the gift he came to offer. All Christian spirituality and ethics must be rooted in Christ; modelled on Christ's life, death, and resurrection; and centered on him.

The concept of *theosis* as a way of understanding the

Christian life is not foreign to the Roman Catholic tradition, although it is an emphasis that has been obscured in the West since the patristic period. Perhaps contemporary efforts to rediscover the distinctively Christian and theological roots of moral theology and of spirituality—together with the renewal of trinitarian studies and a renewed attention to the relationship of the three-Personed God with humanity—can help us to rediscover the importance of *theosis* for an understanding of the moral and spiritual lives of all Christians. In the end, it is sharing in the life of God that is the very purpose and meaning of human life, of goodness, and of holiness—and thus of Christian theology, ethics, and spirituality.

The Christian Life in Relationship

5

AUTHENTIC RELATIONSHIPS: JUSTICE AND LOVE

The letter of James reminds Christians that an authentic Christian faith cannot be completely separated from works:

> What good is it, my brothers and sisters, if you say you have faith but do not have works? Can faith save you? If a brother or sister is naked and lacks daily food, and one of you says to them, "Go in peace; keep warm and eat your fill," and yet you do not supply their bodily needs, what is the good of that? So faith by itself, if it has no works, is dead (Jas 2:14–17 NRSV).

Similarly, a number of theologians have recently suggested that an authentic Christian spirituality cannot be separated from an active concern for and pursuit of justice.[1] These theologians argue that a Christian cannot truly strive to grow in a relationship with God without a real concern for the well-being of other persons. One cannot hope to attain a transcendent union with God without a lived concern for the present circumstances of other men and women.

The present chapter attempts to offer further insight into the connection between justice and spirituality by focusing on the relational aspect of each and by viewing them in light of a contemporary understanding of Christian love. In short, it will be argued that justice, love, and Christian spirituality are all concerned with the establishment of authentic relationships with God, with other persons, and with the created order—ultimately as a transcendent hope but also as a task in present historical circumstances. Thus, while earlier chapters have focused primarily but not exclusively on the life of individual Christians, in this chapter we broaden our perspective to look at the shape of ongoing Christian conversion in relational terms.

The chapter proceeds through the following steps: (1) Justice will be examined from a biblical perspective as the pursuit of "right relationship," a perspective that is given greater specificity by the modern Roman Catholic tradition on justice. (2) A perspective on Christian love as the pursuit of mutuality will suggest a close link with justice understood as "right relationship." (3) It will be suggested that Christian spirituality aims precisely at a relationship of mutual love within the triune life of God but also with other persons in God. (4) The final major section will offer an explication of the relationship between justice and spirituality that follows from the foregoing discussion.

Justice as "Right Relationship"

Contemporary Christian perspectives on justice are returning to a greater focus on biblical views of justice. While recognizing that there is no *one* understanding of justice that is entirely consistent throughout all of the books of the Bible, John Donahue concludes that biblical justice is most basically concerned with "fidelity to the demands of a relationship."[2] In the Bible, the various Hebrew and Greek words that can be translated into English as "justice" are largely relational terms. Justice fundamentally concerns fidelity to relationships—first of all, God's fidelity to the relationships that God has freely entered into with humanity and with the created order. Only after consideration of *divine* faithfulness does "justice" concern *human* fidelity in relationships with God, with other persons, and with the earth.

Justice in the Bible, then, is first and foremost predicated of God: God is just in God's faithful ruling over all that God has created and in the divine fidelity to the covenant that God has graciously offered. God's justice focuses especially on those who are on the margins of the covenanted community that God has called together—such as widows, orphans, sojourners—because the possibility of their participation in the community is threatened precisely by their marginalization. Justice, then, most fundamentally "deals with God's positive actions in creating and preserving community, particularly on behalf of those who are marginal."[3]

It is important to see that the biblical concept of justice is closely related to God's steadfast love *(hesed)*. God's relationship with God's people is not only faithful, but it is characterized at the same time by God's gracious kindness and loving mercy (see Hos 2:19, Is 16:5, Ps 38:4–5). God's justice and God's steadfast love are not contrasting realities but closely associated with one another.[4] This is an important insight in regard to the discussion of justice and love which follows.

From a biblical perspective, human persons are "just" to the extent that they are faithful to the demands of their relationship with God. Such fidelity includes worship and obedience toward God but also includes fidelity to other human persons within the context of covenant and even to those outside of covenant such as resident aliens and sojourners. And just as God's concern focuses on the poor and marginalized, so too should the just nation and just persons focus on concern for the marginalized and threatened—not only in the sense of providing relief from serious want but also in the sense of assisting them in attaining relationships of true equality within the community. Justice is more than meeting needs; God's people must be concerned with enabling the poor to enter into "right relationships," to attain justice, because this is a demand of their relationship with God who is so concerned. The prophetic message calls the people back to the authentic demands of their relationship with God and with one another.[5]

The gospel theme of the reign of God also highlights the establishment of "right relationships" between human persons and God, and extending to the created order. The final realization of God's reign will mean rightly ordered relationships according to God's loving will as manifest in Jesus. The present realization of the reign of God involves the overturning of those aspects of the human condition which hinder the full personal and social development of human persons, whether because of individual sin or because of the oppression of persons through unjust structures. The reign of God aims at "right relationships."[6] Justice, then, involves the "making right" of human relationships with God and with other persons in anticipation of the final realization of God's reign at the parousia.

Biblical perspectives on justice have been profitably incorporated by contemporary liberation theologies. Latin American liberation theology seeks authentic liberation as the overcoming of structures that marginalize and oppress the poor and as the establishment of renewed "right relationships" between oppressed and oppressors according to the will of the God who always seeks liberation for all people. Ultimately the goal is the attainment of true reconciliation and peace between oppressor and oppressed but only as the result of relationships "made right." A lasting order of peace is built on such justice. Similarly, feminist theology seeks right relationships based on equality and aiming ultimately at true mutuality in relationships. This is the positive goal which grounds the feminist critique of patriarchy as the perpetuation of skewed relationships between men and women.

Contemporary liberation theologies further the biblical view of justice by insisting that the establishment of right relationships in contemporary society requires the overturning of structures and institutions that perpetuate oppressive and marginalizing relationships. The maintenance of unjust, inauthentic relationships is not the result only—nor even primarily—of ill will and conscious malice but rather of structures that have been developed over time. In short, liberation theologies insist that the pursuit of justice, of right relationships, in the modern world requires the overcoming of social and structural sin.

A still broader aspect of viewing justice as right relationships is provided by contemporary reflections on ecological justice.[7] Right relationships must be established not only with God and with other human persons but also with the entire created order, with the earth. Respect for the earth is an important aspect of respecting its creator since the created order mediates God's presence. In this sense, the earth can be called sacramental. But respect for the earth is also an important aspect of respecting other persons for whom the earth was created and who likewise depend on its resources. Ecological concern seeks right relationships with the people with whom we now share the earth and its resources and with those who will come after us seeking a share in the earth's goods, its beauty, and its sacramental mediation of God. This is consistent with the concern for the land which marked the Hebrew scriptures and which characterized Israel's fidelity to its covenantal relationship with God and with one another.[8]

It is within the context of a biblical view of justice that we can reappropriate the long-standing Roman Catholic tradition on justice.[9] Justice, according to this natural law tradition, requires rendering to each person his or her due *(suum cuique)*. The actual demands of justice, the identification of what is actually due to each person, are derived largely from reflection on the nature of the human person in his or her multiple relationships. Attention to these multiple relationships yields the various types of justice: commutative (individual to individual), distributive (society to individual), and social (individual to society and to the common good).

The contemporary Roman Catholic understanding of justice, reflecting a broader understanding of the human person and the recognition of contemporary obstacles to integral human development, has emphasized authentic participation as essential to the realization of justice.[10] Justice is not met simply by meeting basic human needs but requires enabling people to participate actively in society. With liberation theologies, then, the contemporary Roman Catholic view of justice attends to structural obstacles to the realization of full human personhood, that is, to structures which oppress, marginalize, and deny authentic participation. The modern Roman Catholic understanding of justice, therefore, is implicitly concerned with the establishment of the conditions which make "right relationships" possible.

In sum, the biblical and modern Roman Catholic views of justice can be seen to be mutually enriching. The explicitly biblical perspective on justice, for its part, provides the broader perspective which helps to clarify the goal and meaning of rendering to each one's due and of seeking authentic participation. On the other hand, however, the modern Roman Catholic tradition serves to provide greater specificity to justice understood as "right relationship." As Karen Lebacqz has pointed out, to define justice as "right relationship" may be an accurate reflection of its biblical meaning but it does not provide much specificity to the shape of such relationships.[11] It can be suggested that the Roman Catholic view of justice with its attention to reciprocal rights and duties within the context of present historical relationships provides just such specificity. The biblical and the modern Roman Catholic views of justice, then, are not in opposition but are mutually enriching—the former providing the broader meaning of justice, the latter providing tools for identifying its more specific shape.

Love and Justice

Christian understanding of justice as right relationship is closely related to a contemporary understanding of Christian love, and the connection between them, as we shall see, highlights the relationship between justice and spirituality. The precise and quintessential meaning of Christian love has been a topic of a good deal of recent theological and ethical reflection. Gene Outka has provided a helpful analysis of three broad "definitions" of Christian love as equal regard, as self-sacrifice, and as mutuality.[12] The present chapter will take up an understanding of Christian love as a pursuit of true mutuality that can be manifest in different circumstances in the form of equal regard or of self-sacrifice. Obviously, our purpose in the present section cannot be to attain final resolution of disputed points in the understanding of Christian love. It is, rather, to suggest that love understood as the pursuit of mutuality can shed light on the meaning of both justice and spirituality and on their relationship with one another.

Human love is grounded in the inherent human drive for self-transcendence which characterizes the human person as embodied spirit created in the image of God. Authentic human development moves along a path of greater transcendence of merely selfish, egocentric interest. Any authentic human loving is therefore necessarily other-directed, other-regarding. Christian love is that love enabled by and modelled after the gift of God's gratuitous self-giving as manifest most perfectly in Jesus Christ. Christians seek to love as God has loved them, with a self-giving modelled on the self-giving of Christ in the event of the cross. Christian love, then, is the manifestation of Christian conversion—that is, the other-worldly falling in love that responds to God's gift of love and that flows out into love for others in affective conversion.

As love modelled after and enabled by divine love, Christian love aims at *mutual* self-giving, at mutuality or communion, since this is the love which characterizes the relationships within the life of the Trinity. The three Persons of the Trinity give and receive love in a relationship of perfect mutuality. It is precisely in the image of the triune God that humankind has been created, and for participation in triune life that humankind has been redeemed. As images of God, mutual self-giving in love is our origin; as creatures called to participate in the triune life of God (*theosis*), mutual self-giving in love is our goal; as followers of the incarnate Son of God, our task in the present is to create the possibility of true mutual self-giving in our interpersonal relationships with God and with others and in the structural relationships of societal life. This character of aiming at mutuality is implied by St. Thomas' assertion that charity is essentially friendship with God (*ST* IIa-IIae, 23.1) in which mutuality is made possible by God's gift in transforming the soul (*ST* IIa-IIae, 23.2).[13] Christian love, then, aims at mutuality with other persons and ultimately with God.

It must be noted immediately that, in the present order, true mutual love is not fully attainable, especially in social relationships, and self-giving love cannot be dependent on the actual promise or expectation of reciprocity from the other. It is for this reason that some prefer to define Christian love in present existence as equal regard—that is, a lived concern for the benefit of others equal to the concern that one legitimately holds for oneself. Equal regard, then, involves a true and active concern for the other but requires no presupposition nor expectation of reciprocity. The definition of love as equal regard, therefore, offers a realistic view of the actual limits of love in a finite world touched by sin.

Still, despite its advantages, equal regard does not seem adequately to encompass love's true goal of mutuality, especially as one looks to the quintessence of love in trinitarian loving. The caution that mutuality is not fully attainable does, however, lead us to define Christian love in present historical circumstances as *at least* equal regard always in *pursuit* of mutuality, rather than as the actual attainment of mutuality. Of course, even God's love for the sinner in the present order is a pursuit rather than a final real-ization of mutuality.

Enda McDonagh offers further insight into equal regard as an aspect of the pursuit of mutuality by cautioning that the emphasis on love as mutuality must not lose the sense of love's recognition of the other *as* other. Love requires a proper sense of differentiation—of "otherness"—or, we might say, of equal regard. Love includes a real sense of "letting the other be," not in a sense of uninterested *laissez-faire* but rather taking seriously the other *as* other and in willing both the other person and oneself to grow into one's own unique fullness.[14] Equal regard, then, is an aspect of the pursuit of mutuality; it is a presupposition, a necessary precondition, for a genuine mutual self-giving; but it is not in itself the proper definition of Christian love. In fact, equal regard bears more directly on justice as right relationship as a necessary foundation for the pursuit of true mutuality.

It is also true that when love-aiming-at-mutuality encoun-ters the refusal of love (sin), it can take the form of self-sacrifice since love always retains its character of self-giving and other-regarding. The cross is, of course, the perfect manifestation of a complete self-giving in love in the face of sin, that is, in the face of a refusal of a *mutual* self-giving. It is no wonder that many have pondered the cross and come to understand self-sacrifice as the quintessence of Christian love. Even the self-sacrifice of the cross, however, aims implicitly at a final mutuality with the other. In his saving death, Jesus does manifest a perfectly self-sacrificial form of love in the face of sin; but, at the same time, the sacrifice of the cross aims ultimately at mutuality since through it God seeks the reconciliation of humanity with God. In the cross, God makes human participation in triune mutuality possible. This is the ultimate meaning of the self-sacrifice of Jesus on the cross when viewed in light of the resurrection, from which it cannot be separated.

Despite the fact that Christian love can take the form of self-sacrifice after the model of the cross, it is important to see, nonetheless, that Christian loving aiming at authentic mutuality is not self-sacrificial in every situation. There are situations in which the good of another person or even one's own good requires the upholding of rights and the overturning of structures that prevent others from attaining full human development and authentic human relationships. At times, the pursuit of authentically mutual relationships requires the refusal to sacrifice, since sacrifice may actually undermine the conditions for the possibility of attaining true mutuality. In such circumstances, Christian love is not self-sacrificing but rather offers real opposition to injustice and sin and makes concrete demands leading to action—that is, Christian love seeks the realization of the conditions necessary to attain right (just) relationships.[15]

Once Christian love has been understood to aim at mutuality, its relationship with justice understood as the effort to attain right relationship becomes clear.[16] Precisely because it aims at mutuality, Christian love always seeks those conditions in which authentic mutuality can occur. For this reason, Christian love always seeks the establishment of right relationships and the overturning of structures and institutions that hinder a genuine mutuality. For the Christian who has come to believe in God's love and who strives to model his or her life after the divine love incarnate in Jesus, justice is a real if incomplete form that love takes in a world of limit and sin.

Christian love, therefore, always seeks justice; but Christian love is never content with the establishment of "mere" justice, seeking rather the establishment of fully mutual relationships.

Any attainment of justice always remains challenged by love to a further attainment. Love as self-giving aimed at mutuality seeks justice but is never exhausted by it. Right (just) relationships are a condition for the realization of fully mutual (loving) relationships but the latter are not exhausted by the former. As John Langan has argued:

> Justice as transformed by charity must not be less than justice. Charity, however, also moves the agent to a good that transcends the good of right social order that justice aims at, and so a person who works for justice in a spirit of charity uses and interprets his work for justice as a stage to a more intimate and loving communion with other persons and with God.[17]

Christian love and its active pursuit of justice in present historical circumstances necessarily seeks the overturning of sin as alienation both from God and from other persons. As the early chapters of Genesis make clear, the rupture of authentic relationship with God is closely related to skewed relationships between and among human persons and between humanity and the earth. The sin of Adam and Eve leads to skewed relationships between men and women and alienation from the rest of creation (Gen 3:16–20) and begins further manifestations of alienation: Cain's murder of his brother, Abel (Gen 4:8–16); the exaggerated revenge of Lamech (Gen 4:22–23); the confusion of languages and the separation of peoples after Babel (Gen 11:1–9). Skewed relationships with God affect human relationships; and the effort to overcome ruptured relationships with God (sin) necessarily includes the effort to attain right (just) relationships with other human persons aiming ultimately at fully mutual (loving) relationships.

The effort to attain justice within the complexities of the modern world makes clear that the alienation that comes from sin requires structural transformation. Sin is not only personal but also social and structural. Justice as the effort to attain right relationships, empowered by love's effort to attain truly mutual relationships, necessarily opposes sin in its interpersonal as well as in its structural forms.

It is precisely in this context that we can see how, from a Thomistic perspective, love is the "form" of the virtue of justice (*ST* IIa-IIae, 23.8). Justice as the disposition to render to each what is due is redirected and perfected by love to the attainment of friendship with God. The Christian who is striving to live an authentic Christian love aiming at mutuality with God and with other persons has new insight into and new reason to seek the foundation of right (just) relationships with other persons. Justice becomes the outward expression of charity, and the precepts of justice become the love's proper channels.[18]

Love and Christian Spirituality

Spirituality, like love, is grounded in the inherent human drive for self-transcendence. The human person as embodied spirit is so constituted that he or she inherently seeks to transcend self, ultimately to attain a relationship of mutuality with God. Our hearts are, as St. Augustine said, restless until they rest in God. Spirituality manifests the fact that human persons were created for loving God, for friendship with God—that is, for a relationship of mutuality with and within the triune life of God.

Christian spirituality, flowing from Christian faith, is more particularly the effort to integrate one's entire life through self-transcendence aiming at communion with God. This life of self-transcending love is made possible by God's free self-giving in Christ and by the ongoing work of the Holy Spirit within the life of the church.[19] Christian spirituality, then, is the entire life of the Christian who seeks to integrate self into the attainment of a relationship of mutuality, communion, friendship with God. Christian spirituality is the life of Christian love which aims at participating fully in trinitarian loving.

Christian spirituality clearly encompasses such traditional elements as prayer, meditation, and contemplation as these aim at a deeper relationship with God. But to see communion with the triune God as the goal of Christian spirituality is already to imply that spirituality is precisely social and communal.[20] Participation in the divine life will not be "me-and-God" but "us-and-God," "us-in-God." The mutuality to be attained in triune

life is not only between human persons and God but also
between and among humans. Christian spirituality, then, is
fundamentally relational in seeking authentic relationships not
only with God but also with other human persons. A number of
New Testament texts and themes make abundantly clear the
intimate connection between seeking authentic relationship with
God and with other persons.

The double command of love (Mk 12:29–31; Mt 22:37–40;
Lk 10:27)—to love God and neighbor—implies the important
interconnection between the love of God and love of human
persons. The first letter of John makes the essential relationship
between the two loves more explicit:

> Those who say, "I love God," and hate their brothers or
> sisters, are liars; for those who do not love a brother or sister
> whom they have seen, cannot love God whom they have not
> seen. The command we have from him is this: those who
> love God must love their brothers and sisters also (1 Jn
> 4:20–21 NRSV).

There is no authentic love for God without love of neighbor.
There is no authentic search for relationship with God—no
authentic Christian spirituality—without a search for authentic
relationship with other human persons.

In fact, the Christian effort to love God is grounded in the
grateful acknowledgement of God's gratuitous love—God's free
offer of relationship. Christian love of neighbor is one aspect of
the Christian's overflowing gratitude for the love that God has
offered: "In this is love, not that we have loved God but that he
loved us and sent his Son to be the atoning sacrifice for our sins.
Beloved, since God loved us so much, we also ought to love one
another" (1 Jn 4:10–11 NRSV). The Christian can only respond to
God fully by gratefully loving brother or sister, and a spirituality
that aims at loving union with God is essentially focused on
loving other persons as well.

Similarly the judgment scene in the gospel of Matthew
(25:31–46) makes clear that the Christian's relationship with
Christ is necessarily mediated in relationships with other

persons, most especially those in need. One cannot seek some "transcendent" relationship with Christ separate from attention to one's neighbor. Final and ultimate communion with God is unattainable for one who does not seek right (just) relationships with other persons.

Finally, the New Testament image of the reign of God implies a Christian spirituality that seeks not only authentic relationship with God but also with other persons. The symbol of God's reign suggests that the ultimate destiny of humanity is social and communal, implying not only authentic relationship with God but also with other human persons. It is for this reason that the church, the community of disciples, seeks to manifest the reign of God by witnessing to authentic, "right," relationships within the Christian community itself. Further, the "present but not yet" nature of God's reign suggests that any authentic Christian spirituality that seeks to conform the Christian life to its ultimate destiny cannot bypass real concern for the quality of actual relationships in the present.

Christian spirituality which aims at a relationship of mutual love with God and in God—and with other persons in the context of triune life—necessarily aims at loving relationship with other persons in the present. In fact, authentic relationships with other persons is the mark of an authentic relationship with God and thus of a genuinely Christian spirituality. This connection is made clear in the Gospel of Matthew: "So when you are offering your gift at the altar, if you remember that your brother or sister has something against you, leave your gift there before the altar and go; first be reconciled to your brother or sister, and then come and offer your gift (Mt 5:23–24 NRSV)." And to see that Christian spirituality aims at authentic relationships with God and with other human persons is to say that it is opposed to sin as that which refuses such relationships, violates them, or permits conditions which make such relationships impossible to attain.

Contemporary ecological spirituality further broadens the relational understanding of Christian spirituality. The Christian loves the creator in caring for the creation that mediates the divine presence. The Christian loves the neighbor in cherishing the earth upon which all persons, present and future, depend for sustenance. Christian spirituality, therefore, attends to the created order as an integral part of the hoped for future of union with God.

Spirituality and Justice

As the present study has attempted to demonstrate, there is no authentic Christian spirituality without active concern for justice. One cannot authentically seek loving union with God without seeking right (just) relationships with other persons as the essential foundation and anticipation of the fully mutual relationships to be realized in the divine life. Active concern for justice provides the necessary foundation for Christian spirituality. Concern for justice, then, does not simply derive from Christian spirituality but is essential to it. Prayer *and* action for justice, contemplation *and* action, are essential to the Christian life, to Christian spirituality.

The justice that Christian spirituality seeks, moreover, is especially focused in its concern for the poor, because the Christian seeks a relationship with a God who has consistently revealed a particular concern for those who are denied right relationships with other persons. Christian spirituality seeks justice for the marginalized because its God is a God of justice, a God of the poor. Spirituality, as Christian, is linked with justice for the poor because Jesus identified himself with the marginalized, with the poor, with victims of injustice. Seeking authentic relationships with God and with other men and women, Christians seek out those whose participation in such relationships is most threatened—those marginalized by oppression and by sin.

Living the Christian life aiming at loving union with God gives new power to the pursuit of justice. The movement of self-transcendence in love which characterizes the Christian "spiritual life" gradually frees the Christian from the selfish desires and attachments that are at the root of injustice and of blindness to it. More particularly, prayer and contemplation give new perspectives on, and new freedom from, the accepted patterns of relationships, freeing the person of prayer to be a critical observer of accepted and currently acceptable patterns of human existence. As Terry Tastard states:

> Contemplative love of God pulls people out of their comfortable rut. It makes them reject formulas which explain away the plight of the poor or which dismiss the clouds of war. God's uncompromising love shows up human compromises, it illuminates and throws into sharp relief the standards we judge by, and this is true both for those who have previously been committed to social justice and those who have not. This, I think, is why Merton says that the more we love God the more we will become disturbing people.[21]

Perhaps one of the best contemporary examples of the power of prayer and contemplation to give critical vision is Thomas Merton himself, who was both a contemplative monk and an astute social critic.[22]

But if Christian spirituality provides new power to active concern for justice, it is no less true that pursuit of justice provides an ongoing challenge for Christian spirituality. While biblical faith has given Latin American, feminist, and ecological theologians perspectives from which to pursue the realization of justice, it is also true that their pursuit of justice has given them perspectives from which to criticize inauthentic elements of and developments in Christian spirituality. Those who wholeheartedly seek right (just) relationships with other people possess important insights into the foundation of any relationship that seeks to be truly mutual, genuinely loving—just as those who wholeheartedly seek authentic loving relationships with God and others strive more earnestly for the attainment of justice.

Each Christian, therefore, in striving to live an authentic Christian life must seek *both* a holistic spiritual growth *and* the attainment of justice. The integration of these aspects of the Christian life will be realized differently in each Christian's actual life depending on circumstances and vocation, but no Christian is exempt from the pursuit of both. There is no authentic Christian spirituality without active concern for justice; the pursuit of justice, on the other hand, is denied its fullest meaning and purpose without Christian spirituality.

Conclusion

As a number of different theologians have pointed out, one biblical text perhaps best captures the relationship of justice, love, and spirituality: "…and what does the Lord require of you but to do justice, and to love kindness, and to walk humbly with your God?" (Mic 6:8 NRSV).[23] Walter Brueggemann has described this verse as "a focal summary of prophetic faith, prophetic hope and prophetic challenge,"[24] and he goes on to demonstrate that all three "requirements" are intimately and essentially interrelated with one another: justice, love, and walking with God.[25] All three provisions are ultimately relational, and together they point to the intimate connection of love, justice, and relationship with God.

What the Lord requires is that we do justice, love kindness, and walk humbly with our God. To seek justice without love would result in a sterile and minimalistic realization of justice. To strive to love without an active pursuit of justice would reduce love to little more than a sentiment. To seek either or both without striving to grow in an authentic relationship with God emaciates both by depriving them of their ultimate meaning, goal, and source of power.

A holistic Christian spirituality, the whole Christian life, aims at attaining authentic relationship with God, with other persons and with the whole created order. Christian spirituality, then, requires justice even as it aims at a full mutuality in love. Love, justice, and Christian spirituality are distinct but inseparable aspects of the Christian response to God who has first invited humanity into relationship with and within God's own triune life.

6

LITURGY AND CHRISTIAN LIVING

The Second Vatican Council taught that the liturgy is both the "fount" and "summit" of the church's activities and of the Christian life.[1] It is no surprise, then, that many theologians have maintained that the Christian spiritual life is rooted in the liturgy.[2] One's personal prayer is intimately connected with the communal prayer of the church's liturgy. No less does the Christian moral life find its fount and summit in the celebration of the liturgy, although far less attention has been focused on this relationship. In this chapter we will be examining the vital connection between liturgy and morality—and implicitly, therefore, the connection between a liturgical spirituality and moral living.

In the pages that follow we will first look broadly at the relationship between liturgy and morality within the wider context of Christian life and theology. We will then focus at greater length on *how* the liturgy influences the moral life and then on *how* good moral living impacts the celebration of the liturgy. Finally, we will look more narrowly at the important relationship of liturgy and justice.

Liturgy and Morality

As we have already noted in earlier chapters, Bernard Häring has insisted, throughout his writings and over many years, that the Christian life must be understood as a response to God's self-offer in Christ and to God's invitation to relationship.[3] The religious response of faith and the moral response of good living, says Häring, are linked as the two basic forms of the Christian's fundamental response to God. So too, then, are prayer/worship/sacrament related and interconnected with moral living as two forms of the Christian response to God's gracious self-offering in Christ. It is likely that this holistic vision of moral living is one aspect of the broader shape of the Christian life that may explain, at least in part, the large number of spiritual and sacramental writings by a moral theologian such as Häring.[4] Häring's work suggests for us that we first look to the most basic character of Christian life as a grateful response to God as a most basic link between liturgy and morality.

The interconnection of liturgy and moral living has also been suggested implicitly by our earlier discussion of conversion as the foundation of the Christian moral and spiritual life. This is so because the celebration of the liturgy is itself rooted in Christian conversion.[5] Those who have experienced an "other-worldly falling in love" with the God of Jesus Christ assemble to express their gratitude for the love that was first revealed and poured forth on them. They gather in the liturgy to celebrate, to confirm, and to nourish their communal and personal life in Christ—that is, to celebrate, confirm and nourish their ongoing conversion through spiritual and moral growth. For those who have not yet experienced the true "falling in love" of Christian conversion, participation in the liturgy is an ever renewed invitation to a total surrender to God without qualification or reservation. Therefore, the Christian liturgy is a celebration of the experience of conversion already realized; it is an empowerment and nourishment for ongoing conversion in moral and spiritual striving; and it is an invitation to the total surrender of Christian conversion for those who have not yet experienced it.

The Christian tradition has long expressed the connection between prayer/liturgy and belief/theology in terms of the principle *lex orandi, lex credendi*—the law of prayer is the law of belief (and the law of belief is the law of prayer). Of course, to suggest, as we have, that Christian faith and theology as well as Christian liturgy and spirituality are rooted in the experience of conversion, is already to provide the essential foundation for the connection between the *lex orandi* and *lex credendi*. Protestant ethicist Paul Ramsey suggested the expansion of this ordering to include, on an equal basis, *lex bene operandi*, thus: the law of prayer is the law of belief is the law of acting well. It is in the relationship of this ordering that Ramsey grounds the link between liturgy and ethics.[6] To speak of an essential interrelationship among prayer, theology and action is certainly consistent with the contemporary insistence of liberation theologies that orthodoxy (right thinking—more literally, of course, "right praise") is inseparable from orthopraxis (right action).[7]

The foregoing discussion has tried to establish, in broad strokes, that Christian moral and spiritual lives are closely linked with the liturgy. In the two sections that follow we will examine *how* liturgy and morality impact one another—first how liturgy influences the moral life and then how moral living impacts the liturgy.

Liturgy Shaping Christian Life

The liturgy shapes the Christian moral life in a rich variety of interrelated ways. In sum, we might say that the liturgy allows the Christian to encounter God and to participate in God's saving deeds as these are recalled, celebrated, and made present in the Christian story. This encounter and participation forms in the Christian a distinctively Christian vision of reality and of oneself in relation to God, to others and to creation. The liturgy, then, forms the Christian's understanding and affect in a way that has vitally important ramifications for moral action and living. It is precisely the multifaceted effects of liturgical participation that we will be examining in this section.

Participation in the Christian Story

In the liturgy, the Christian community gathers to recall and to celebrate the foundational stories of its faith, most especially the stories of Jesus. The communal remembering is central to the celebration of the liturgy. It puts Christians in touch with God's saving action in the past, releasing the power of the past into the present and breaking open new possibilities in the present and into the future.[8] Remembering within the context of the liturgy is therefore not a sterile recall of a disconnected past nor the mere recollection of moral or religious heroes and heroines for the sake of pious imitation. Rather, liturgical remembering functions symbolically so that Christians actually participate in the power of the stories made present and are thereby renewed, challenged, formed, and nourished.

To "participate" in the celebration of the liturgy is far more than joining in the singing or even exercising some liturgical ministry. Liturgical participation means participating in the history of God's saving deeds and encounters with God's people. Most especially, it means entering into the paschal mystery of Christ's dying and rising and so to be transformed by it into newness of life.[9] Participation in the Christian liturgy marks one's life with the sign of the cross in living hope of the resurrection. Those who celebrate the liturgy are transformed by—in order to live—the self-giving of Christ manifest in the paschal mystery. Timothy Sedgwick suggests that the liturgy forms Christians in a "paschal identity" and that the task of Christian ethics, therefore, is precisely to describe the pattern of this paschal form of living.[10]

The power of sacramental liturgy to disclose, make present, and celebrate the reality of the past challenges Christians themselves to live sacramentally. The liturgy challenges Christians to disclose, reveal, and celebrate God's presence in their daily lives as they have experienced it in the liturgy.[11] The sacramental nature of the Christian life has important implications for the moral life. It is certainly not possible simply to derive moral duties from an understanding of the Christian life as sacramental in character, but there are some attitudes and actions that do seem readily to disclose the presence of God in the world, while others cannot. The celebration of the sacramental liturgy, then, nourishes sacramental lives that disclose God's presence, in part, through good moral actions.

A Christian Vision of Reality

Participation in the liturgy and the stories it celebrates comes to shape the Christian's view of reality itself. Regular liturgical remembering of the Christian stories causes these stories to become increasingly normative for the Christian's understanding of self, others, and world. They come to provide the interpretive lens through which the world is viewed and understood. One's vision of reality—of self, others, and world—has an important impact on how one assesses and acts in situations of choice. We shall examine below the importance of a Christian vision in our discussion of the moral imagination.

Timothy Sedgwick has suggested that the foundational stories of the Christian faith function both mythically and parabolically.[12] Liturgical remembering functions mythically in explaining reality and thereby mediating a world both to the individual and to the community. Liturgy, therefore, helps to construct a reality, providing a stable lens from which Christians come to view the world around them. At the same time, liturgical remembering functions parabolically in that, like the parables of Jesus, the stories celebrated in the liturgy constantly challenge the prevailing vision of the individuals and community. Participative remembering in the liturgy continually breaks open one's worldview and reveals new possibilities for understanding and action in the world.

Christian Identity

One vitally important aspect of the Christian vision formed by the liturgy involves an understanding of one's own identity. We come to understand ourselves and our relationship to God, to others, and to the world in the context of the reality revealed to us in the liturgy. More specifically, we come to understand ourselves within the context of participative remembering. The living memory of Jesus in particular, and of his self-giving life and death for others, helps to form the identity of those who wish to follow him as his disciples. Memory, and in this case liturgical remembering, is vitally important to one's self-identity. Margaret Mary Kelleher notes that to lose one's memory means a loss of identity: "Without memory we don't know who we are. As we develop and change over a lifetime we draw on the past and integrate it into the present through the combined activities of

memory and imagination."[13] Liturgy puts Christians in touch
with the living memory of the Christian community as they form
their identity as disciples in the world.

Just as one's vision of reality will affect one's assessment of a
situation and therefore one's decisions, so too one's understanding of oneself influences the courses of action that one will
consider as most consistent with one's self-identity. Christians
come to each situation with this often implicit understanding
of themselves formed after the model of Jesus and others
encountered in the liturgy. For example, they may see themselves
as a "person for others" or as a "minister of reconciliation," or
perhaps as an agent of justice after the model of some of the
prophets; and this self-identity impacts how they will respond in
the situation itself. They will have a disposition to be of service to
others or to bring reconciliation in the midst of conflict or perhaps
to denounce injustice at any cost to self.

The Christian story celebrated in the liturgy also helps to
give shape and direction to one's positive fundamental option,
that is, to one's identity as a person who has directed his or her
life to communion with God. As we have seen in our earlier
discussion of fundamental option, this requires ongoing integration and direction. In coming to a Christian vision and self-
identity, Christians give shape to their effort to integrate all of
their dispositions and actions into their most fundamental life
direction. Participation in the liturgy, then, confirms one's option
for the God encountered there and provides direction for this
option. The liturgy teaches the Christian what it means to be a
person whose life is oriented to God.

Looking at the question of Christian identity from the
perspective of deification, also discussed in an earlier chapter, we
see that participation in the liturgy has an important impact on
one's life of *theosis*, of sharing in the divine life. In the liturgy,
Christians enter into the triune life in a privileged way; they
participate in the "heavenly liturgy." In so doing they anticipate
the future that God holds in store for them, but they also celebrate
the present reality of their graced sharing in trinitarian life. In the
liturgy, Christians are powerfully reminded of their identity as
people whom God has invited to participate in God's own inner

life, not only in a distant future but even in the present. Liturgical participation in the divine life, therefore, challenges and empowers Christians to be who they already are and who they are called to be: sharers in trinitarian community.

Philip Rossi focuses his discussion of liturgy and ethics on the power of liturgy to form an authentic vision of ourselves specifically as moral agents. The celebration of the liturgy, says Rossi, serves to debunk the prevailing image of moral agency in contemporary Western culture as a "solitary individual agent who must carry the entire weight of moral existence through the exercise of free choice."[14] This prevailing cultural view skews both the moral life and the understanding of worship since it reduces the human person to a solitary individual, the moral life to a solitary battle, and the liturgy to a private encounter of the individual with God. On the contrary, Rossi argues:

> Worship is the acknowledgement that our lives are not under our autonomous control: they are to take shape in response to God's disclosure of his presence among his people and his will that they be redeemed. The picture of the moral autonomous agent makes it impossible to understand how this agent can make such acknowledgement of God's presence as Lord of life; it makes it impossible to make intelligible or to ground the conviction that Christian moral life is given shape by and in the presence of the living God.[15]

It is the understanding of oneself as in relationship with and responsible to God and to others that is formed in Christian worship, and it is this worship-based identity that can form authentic Christian moral living and action.

Moral Perception and Imagination

The liturgy gives shape not only to one's self-identity but also to how one perceives the situations in which choices are to be made. It does so especially through the formation of a Christian moral imagination.[16] It is the moral imagination that allows us to perceive the various values and other relevant factors present in concrete situations, and it is the moral imagination that allows us to picture various options for choice and their ramifications. The moral imagination, therefore, plays a vitally important, if often unnoticed, role in decision-making and action.[17]

Further, beyond one's perception and understanding of a situation, the moral imagination motivates and empowers actions in a way that insight alone cannot. The moral imagination is closely tied to one's affective response in situations. As one pictures various options through the imagination, one experiences a sometimes powerful affective response to one or more options, whether of attraction or aversion. While the knowledge of rules and rational analyses are vitally important, moral insight alone—even when clear and certain—often cannot motivate without an accompanying affective response. This is especially true in the face of obstacles and contrary inclinations that can render the agent virtually paralyzed to actually accomplish the good. Moral imagination, then, especially as it impacts one's affective response to value, can more powerfully motivate one to right action.

When, for example, Christians come to a situation of poverty and oppression, they come with a vision of reality formed by the stories of God's preferential concern for the poor. Perhaps they come with a vision of the prophetic condemnation of Israel for ignoring the poor, or perhaps of Jesus attending to the needs of the marginalized. The moral imagination allows the Christian to see the present situation in contrast to the powerfully compelling images of the Christian story. They are able to see, therefore, beyond (without ignoring) mere human rights claims, abstract principles of justice, and rational analyses of the situation; they also see brothers and sisters, people like themselves created and redeemed by God in Christ, and they see options that rational analysis alone might too quickly dismiss. Further, the moral imagination empowers Christians to take the side of the poor even though it involves a threat to their own privilege and comfort.

Revealing Values

Bernard Lonergan, in explicating the relationship between religious and moral conversion, maintained that the gift of God's love in religious conversion "reveals values in their splendor, while the strength of this love brings their realization, and that is moral conversion."[18] Liturgy, rooted in experience of Christian conversion and empowering ongoing conversion, helps to teach authentic values as these are revealed in the Christian stories. The Christian apprehension and appreciation of values is tutored by the liturgy so that these values can be sought in daily living.[19] In so doing, the celebration of the liturgy offers valuable assistance to actual moral choices and offers an implicit critique of the skewed sense of value present within the Christian and in contemporary society.

Enda McDonagh explains how the liturgy in particular teaches the Christian the value of human persons and their needs.[20] McDonagh argues that the foundational moral experience of human persons is the experience of other persons as gift.[21] Although this experience may not be made explicit or may even be marred by personal and social sin, other human persons are experienced as of unique and irreducible value. It is from this experience of other as gift that there arises the moral "call" to respond appropriately to the value of persons and their needs. This openness to others, McDonagh argues, is already potentially an openness to the divine Other. Liturgy focuses, explicates, and celebrates other human persons- -and indeed the whole created order—as created, loved, and redeemed by God in Christ. Liturgy, therefore, lends new power to the foundational response to other persons that is the heart of all good moral action. Further, in the liturgy, Christians acknowledge and celebrate one another as sons and daughters of God and thus as brothers and sisters to one another. People who participate in the celebration of the liturgy, then, are empowered to see other persons as gift with a greater clarity and to respond to their needs with a greater urgency.

Christian Character

Much of our discussion of the influence of liturgy on the moral life has suggested the ways in which the liturgy forms a Christian vision and the Christian's perception of self, of particular situations, of various options for choice, and of values.

Our discussion of moral imagination, however, has also suggested the important impact of liturgy on the Christian's affective response in particular situations. The liturgy not only forms and corrects one's understanding, whether of reality or of one's self; it also forms and corrects one's will and one's affect.

In addition to perception and understanding, the liturgy also forms distinctively Christian dispositions, affections, intentions, and motives that empower one to act.[22] The liturgy helps to form a distinctively Christian character and virtues that enable the person to perform the good more readily, more consistently, and with less internal struggle. The person with an authentically Christian character, the possessor of Christian virtues, comes to do the good as by instinct. For the "moral virtuoso," moral living becomes an art, a matter of the heart and intuition, and not only a rational and disciplined effort.

A Caution

It has not been our purpose, in discussing the influence of liturgy on the Christian moral life, to suggest that the celebration of the liturgy alone is sufficient for the formation of morally good Christians. Christian vision, identity, imagination, character, and virtue are not sufficient to lead to sound and justifiable moral conclusions in every concrete situation, especially as the complexity of situations increases. Careful moral reasoning and sound moral teaching are essential to moral formation and decision-making.[23] Nothing in our discussion is meant to deny this fact. At the same time, however, careful moral reasoning and sound moral teaching are also not sufficient in themselves for the formation of morally good Christians nor are they sufficient for good decision-making, as we shall see in the following chapters.

The Moral Life Impacting the Liturgy

Although our major focus in this chapter has been the important role that liturgy plays in forming the Christian moral life, it must also be noted that good moral living has an important impact on the celebration of the liturgy. In this section, we examine three aspects of the influence of good moral living on the liturgy: good moral living "authenticating" the liturgy, the moral life forming those who celebrate the liturgy, and the moral life offering a critique of inauthentic elements in the actual historical celebration of the liturgy.

Authenticating the Liturgy

One of the standard, often mentioned, reasons that nominal Christians might offer for refusing to participate in the liturgy is that they are scandalized by the "hypocrisy" of those who worship on Sunday but who live pagan lives during the rest of the week. Obviously, many responses could be made to such a statement, but it does point to the fact that we commonly expect that participation in the liturgy will, in fact, be manifest in daily living. Failure to live a life authentically formed by the liturgy can make the liturgy seem incredible as a manifestation of Christian faith; and for this reason, moral living can be said to "authenticate" the liturgy.[24] It must be acknowledged that Christians remain imperfect sinners who regularly fall short of moral perfection and the highest of Christian ideals, but it must also be recognized that failure to strive for good moral living raises serious doubts about the authenticity of the individual's participation in the liturgy and perhaps about the authenticity of the community's celebration itself.

Preparing for the Liturgy

More positively, as Enda McDonagh has argued, moral living prepares Christians for the celebration of the liturgy:

> The life which the disciple brings to liturgical performance obviously qualifies his ability to participate, to respond creatively to the divine initiative....The interaction between liturgy and living applies at the level of moral understanding and awareness so that the more developed a disciple is morally, the more fully he is capable of entering into the experience of the liturgy and so increasing his understanding (and performance) of the demands of discipleship.

Liturgy operates then as a source of moral understanding but the understanding it provides is influenced in turn by the prior moral commitment and sensitivity of the participants. The dialectic of theory and praxis which operates in both liturgical and moral awareness and performance is compounded by a dialectic of liturgy and moral living in the life of the disciple.[25]

Earlier, we discussed McDonagh's reflection on the foundational moral experience of other persons as gift. In light of that discussion, we can see that those whose lives manifest a consistent and sensitive response to other persons as gift are better prepared to celebrate other persons as gift and as brothers and sisters in the liturgy. They are better prepared to raise up grateful worship to God in the liturgy for the giftedness of their lives. Good moral living always involves an authentic response to other persons as gift, and thus good moral living prepares the Christian to celebrate a grateful liturgy.

Further, we discussed above Philip Rossi's insistence that the prevailing view of moral agency as the solitary individual confounds the authentic celebration of the liturgy. The prevailing view suggests that the solitary moral agent comes to the liturgy for a private encounter of the individual self and God. In the light of Rossi's reflections, we can suggest that living the moral life, not as a solitary individual but as communal persons in relationship with and responsible to God and to others, enhances the celebration of the communal liturgy. Christian moral agents who understand themselves in relationship to God and others are better prepared to enter into the essentially communal celebration of the liturgy.

Challenging the Liturgy

It will be obvious, of course, that the present discussion of the formative power of the liturgy represents something of an ideal. In fact, for a variety of reasons, as the actual lives of Christians demonstrate, even consistent and heartfelt participation in the liturgy does not result in perfect moral performance. Besides the individual Christian's personal resistances, there is the fact that Christians belong to a number of communities which form them in sometimes competing stories and values.[26] While the Christian strives to make the Christian stories definitively normative in his or her life, this is not easily or quickly accomplished. And just as participation in the Christian story can work subtly but powerfully for good, so too the stories of other communities can also work both subtly and powerfully for good or for ill.

Inauthentic elements brought into the liturgy from other communities and their stories can even find a place in the liturgy itself and be perpetuated there. In actual historical and cultural contexts, social sin such as racism, sexism, classism, or consumerism can infiltrate the actual shape of liturgical celebration. In this case aspects of the actual liturgical performance can obstruct authentic moral formation and can even offer sacral confirmation of such inauthentic elements.[27] We can think, for example, of the way that materialism and consumerism in contemporary society might impact the celebration of the liturgy in a well-to-do parish. In such a situation, the celebration of the liturgy would subtly but powerfully confirm these social sins and further form participants in these false values.

In light of the imperfect and sometimes even skewed communication of the Christian story in the liturgy, good moral living and sound moral reflection can offer an important critique of the actual shape of liturgical structures and performance. The Christian whose life is committed to action on behalf of justice and the option for the poor, for example, is powerfully sensitized to any reflection of inauthentic and unjust relationships that might manifest themselves in liturgical performance. Just as liturgy can offer a critique of the moral living of its participants, so too good moral living and reflection can offer critique of liturgical performance for the sake of a more authentic formation in Christian discipleship.

Liturgy and Justice

There has been a good deal of important reflection on the more narrow area of the relationship of liturgy and justice[28] and of eucharist and justice.[29] It would be impossible to review all of this literature in the context of the present chapter. Nonetheless an overview of some important themes can serve to shed further light on our broader concern for the relationship of liturgy and the moral life in general. Further, it can suggest some important links between the present topic and the discussion in the previous chapter on the relationship of spirituality and justice as the pursuit of authentic relationships.

The relationship of worship and justice is clearly presumed in the scriptures.[30] The covenant between God and the people of Israel required both right worship and right conduct; the two were inseparable. It is precisely in light of the covenant that the prophets decried the separation between cult and conduct:

> I hate, I despise your festivals,
>   and I take no delight in your solemn assemblies.
> Even though you offer me your burnt offerings
>   and grain offerings,
>   I will not accept them;
> and the offerings of well-being of your fatted animals
>   I will not look upon.
> Take away from me the noise of your songs;
>   I will not listen to the melody of your harps.
> But let justice roll down like waters,
>   and righteousness like an everflowing stream.
>   (Amos 5:21–24 NRSV)[31]

Perhaps the clearest connection in the New Testament between eucharist and justice is made by Paul in his condemnation of the celebration of the Lord's supper at Corinth (1 Cor 11:17–33). The division of the wealthy and the poor and the manifestation of factions in the very context of the eucharist threatened its very authenticity. Eugene LaVerdiere comments:

> Paul called the Christians at Corinth to a way of life and a set
> of attitudes that were consistent with the Lord's supper.
> Apart from this way of life, there could be no Lord's supper.
> The prophets had a similar message for Judah and Israel.
> Moral life that was not consistent with their worship made

their worship worthless and even repugnant to God. Like the Lord's supper at Corinth, worship remained such only in name.[32]

The gospel of John offers another powerful witness to the connection of eucharist and service. In the fourth gospel, the institution narrative at the last supper is replaced with the account of Jesus washing the feet of the disciples (Jn 13:1–20). This provides at least a powerful suggestion of the connection between eucharist and service.[33]

Commenting on the witness of the New Testament and post-apostolic period, Hans Bernhard Meyer concludes that the connection between liturgy and service is clear.[34] He notes that many terms used by the early Christian community for social concerns—*diakonia, koinonia, leitourgia, eulogia, kharis, prosphora, thysia, offerre, oblatio, operari*—also had a clearly religious and liturgical character. Meyer suggests that it was precisely the strong connection between worship and morality, worship and social commitment, that made the Christian faith so attractive to pagans since this connection was lacking in the contemporary pagan religions.

The more modern concern for the relationship of liturgy and justice is often associated with the liturgical movement prior to the Second Vatican Council. Certainly one of the most important figures of the liturgical movement in the United States and perhaps the most dedicated to making clear the connection between liturgy and social justice was Virgil Michel (1890–1938).[35] Michel, a Benedictine monk of St. John's Abbey in Collegeville, was the founder of *Orate Fratres* (the forerunner of *Worship*). Seeking the renewal of the liturgy and imbued with the spirit of the growing body of modern Catholic social thought, Michel was insistent that worship and social action cannot be separated. The church that celebrates itself as the "mystical body of Christ" in the eucharist is required to act as Christ's members in the world, manifesting the concern of Jesus for others and especially for the worker and for the poor. The eucharist and the metaphor of the "mystical body of Christ" also played an important role in the spirituality of Dorothy Day and of the early Catholic Worker movement. Sadly, however, by the late 1950s, the cooperation between the liturgical and social apostolates was virtually lost.

The vital concern of Michel and others for the connection between liturgy and justice in the decades prior to the Second Vatican Council makes it particularly odd that the council itself neglects the topic altogether. The council did focus attention both on the liturgy and on the church's social mission in the world, but it did not discuss their interrelationship. John Egan states the problem baldly:

> In this way Vatican II, by its silence, lends sad confirmation to what was a fact of life at the time: the failure of Christian people and Christian leaders to acknowledge the essential connection between liturgy and society, much less liturgy and social justice.[36]

Egan himself argues that the contemporary church is in need of an official pastoral statement that explicitly links the liturgy and social life.[37] Despite the absence of explicit teaching from the council, it is certainly the case nonetheless that the council laid the groundwork from which the connection between liturgy and justice can be made apparent.[38] More recently, the Catholic bishops of the United States devoted a brief section of their 1986 pastoral letter on the U.S. economy to the relationship of worship and action in the world.[39]

The foregoing historical overview has been aimed at suggesting that the relationship of liturgy and justice has its firm roots in the Christian tradition—even if those roots have at times remained hidden. The discussion of spirituality and justice in the previous chapter suggests a more constructive discussion of the relationship of liturgy and justice. There it was proposed that justice is most basically the pursuit of authentic relationships with God, other persons, and with the created order itself. From a Christian perspective, the striving for authentic relationships— for justice—ultimately aims at the full mutuality of trinitarian love.

It is clear that the liturgy presupposes authentic relationships within the celebrating community, and it aims to celebrate and to promote these just relationships.[40] Even more, the liturgy celebrates and anticipates the full mutuality that God offers to men and women in Christ. Fully mutual relationships require just relationships as their precondition. In this light, we can see that liturgy presupposes—requires—just relationships even while it celebrates and points to an ever more complete realization of fully mutual relationships. Where authentic relationships in the community are absent or skewed, the full and authentic celebration of the liturgy is threatened, mitigated, and perhaps even obstructed. Further, where Christians fail to seek the establishment of such relationships even outside the Christian community, the authenticity of their liturgical celebrations is compromised.

To establish the connection between liturgy and authentic relationships is, of course, to point to the relationship between the liturgy and the reign of God.[41] In witnessing and celebrating authentic relationships that aim at mutuality, the liturgy is witnessing and celebrating the coming of God's reign. The liturgy offers a "rehearsal" of the authentic relationships that are to be established in daily living. In fact, the celebration of the liturgy makes Christians better able to recognize the manifestation of the reign of God in history since the shape of God's reign is outlined in the liturgy itself.[42]

Furthermore, more than merely pointing to the reign of God where just and loving relationships will be realized, the liturgy makes the reign of God actually present. Dianne Bergant says:

> ...liturgy not only proclaims and celebrates what has been accomplished but it also announces and anticipates what has not yet been fully realized. In a very real sense, liturgy is itself the very act of establishing the reign of God. It is a sacramental or symbolic act that creates the reality it signifies. It initiates a transformation that is intended to spread beyond the confines of the gathered community.[43]

The celebration of the liturgy, then, as a witness of authentic relationships and of the reign of God has profound social implications. To celebrate the liturgy is to challenge all social, cultural, religious, political, and economic arrangements and structures that do not embody and witness to the authentic relationships modelled in the liturgy. The community that gathers to celebrate the liturgy thereby commits itself to the transformation of their own relationships with the Christian community but also to the transformation of all human relationships whether interpersonal, social, or structural. The celebration of the liturgy therefore challenges both Christians and the world.[44] Archbishop Raymond Hunthausen says:

> During the liturgy we have a glimpse of what the kingdom could be like. While there, we can compare the status quo with the possibilities the kingdom offers us, and we can get up enough nerve to begin changing the way things are in our social and cultural structures, in our politics and economics, in our cities, our streets, and in our neighborhoods.[45]

The celebration of the liturgy impacts and forms the lives of individual Christians; no less does it impact the assembled community; even more, it aims at the transformation of the world.

Conclusion

The Christian life, always both moral and spiritual, is an ongoing journey toward goodness and holiness. Empowered by grace and aided by the support and challenge of one's fellow travellers, it nonetheless requires a lifelong and disciplined effort. The communal celebration of the liturgy is a privileged source of assistance on this life journey and a foretaste of its goal. The liturgy is, as the Second Vatican Council taught, like a fountain of life-giving grace for the Christian journey and for the praise and glory of God.[46]

In this chapter, we have been examining in particular the assistance that the liturgy offers one's moral striving—the Christian effort to become morally good and to establish justice in the world. While acknowledging that the morally good lives of Christians impact the celebration of the liturgy, we have focused especially on the way that the liturgy forms Christians to follow the way of Christ in their daily lives and choices. In the liturgy, sinful men and women encounter the living God; and the living history of God's outpouring of love on the human family is made present. In the liturgy, Christians celebrate the divine love manifest most perfectly in Jesus and effective still through the presence of the Holy Spirit. How could the encounter with such inconceivable love—a love so great that God gave his only Son to save sinners—how could such recollection not call forth a grateful, total, and lifelong response? The Christian moral and spiritual lives are the two aspects of this response, a response that is formed and empowered in the grateful celebration of the church's liturgy.

Christian Life Focused in Decisions

7

PRAYER AND DECISION-MAKING

The suggestion that prayer and moral decision-making are intimately interrelated will not strike the mature Christian as in any way odd. Especially in critical moments of decision, Christians quite naturally turn to God in prayer, asking for guidance and support in making good choices and in carrying them out. But prayer and decision-making are not, need not, and indeed should not be linked only in times of particularly difficult or important decisions. Every situation is an opportunity to further God's loving will for oneself and for others. Every moment is the *kairos*—the "now"—of encounter with God and of response to the divine call. As Christians strive to discover and to do God's will at every moment of their lives, they have reason to be confident in the real though sometimes mysterious guidance of the Holy Spirit made available through prayer.

To accept the link between prayer and decision-making is not in itself problematic, but to describe *how* they are related is a bit more difficult. The Holy Spirit aids the Christian; but how is this assistance "mediated"—that is, how does prayer and the divine assistance impact the course of one's decisions? The present chapter will suggest a number of ways that prayer impacts the moral choices of Christians by influencing men and women as decision-makers. This chapter, then, stands in the middle ground between a broader study of the impact of prayer on the moral life in general[1] and a more narrow study of the role of prayer amid the various other factors that are essential to a good decision[2] (more closely related to the topic of the next chapter). Our immediate concern here is the impact of prayer on the person who decides—how prayer changes the agent who comes to the situation of choice—thereby impacting the decisions themselves. Our discussion in the previous chapter of liturgy and the moral life should provide a useful context for this discussion of personal prayer and decision-making.

While common Christian experience has retained the intuition of the important connection between praying and deciding, their interrelationship is a bit of a rediscovery for Catholic moral theology. In fact, the examination of prayer and decision-making is an important aspect of relating spirituality and ethics, and it serves to focus the broader discussion. This is so because moral decisions give concrete expression to the moral life of the individual (and indirectly to the moral life of the community in which the individual is formed). In a similar way—just as one knows the health of a tree by the fruit it bears— decisions and the actions that flow from them are an important expression of one's spirituality. In fact, a person's actions are one of the most reliable indications of the authenticity of the person's prayer. To examine the relationship of prayer and decision-making is to focus our attention on the most concrete expression of the broader relationship of spirituality and ethics.

For moral theology before the Second Vatican Council, closely linked as it was with canon law, decision-making was largely a matter of obeying laws. A good decision required a knowledge of the relevant laws and rules, an ability to understand the situation in which they were to be applied, and the prudence to deduce one's actual moral obligation from the law applied to the situation. Prayer might have offered a useful addition to this rational, deductive process; but prayer did not seem essential to it.

Contemporary moral theology, on the other hand, is suggesting that the process of deciding must be significantly broader. Laws and rules remain important, but so, too, is the well-formed conscience, one's personal character and virtues, one's commitment to and appropriation of the Christian story and tradition, one's meditation on the word of God, and the working of grace in the daily life of the Christian. All of these will have an important influence on the choices that one makes. In some situations, laws and rules readily apply to provide rather clear direction to one's decisions; but in many other situations, laws do not exist or they cannot easily be applied to a complex situation. A number of Catholic and Protestant ethicists are discussing the importance of "discernment" in good decision-making.[3] Discernment, the discovery of God's will in concrete situations, has long been a theme of Catholic spirituality. It is now being suggested—as the next chapter will show—as an important link between the Christian's spiritual and moral life and as an important context for Christian decision-making.

It is within the context of the "rediscovery" of prayer by Catholic moral theology that the present chapter will suggest how prayer impacts Christian moral decision-making—not only prayer in the actual situation of choice but, more basically, a *life* of prayer. In particular, it will suggest how various, particular "stances" or "attitudes" in prayer impact the Christian as a decision-maker in everyday life. These "stances" in prayer—whether of gratitude, repentance, communion, petition—are not mutually exclusive. People of prayer approach God from different perspectives and with different attitudes as their situations, moods, and needs change—just as, in our relation ships with other human persons, we can take different postures within the context of a single friendship: sometimes grateful, sometimes repentant, sometimes listening, sometimes request-ing. Since each of these stances is simply a different interior posture in prayer within the context of one's whole relationship with God, they are not meant to be mutually exclusive nor are their influences on Christian choices to be considered distinct and separate. In fact, the broader purpose of this chapter is to suggest that a *life* of prayer, taken up from various perspectives and attitudes, changes the Christian as a moral agent. Largely for the sake of greater cohesiveness, we will arrange these stances under two broad headings: prayer as response and prayer as communion.

Prayer as Response

The Christian life itself is always a response to God who offers the divine life and love to the people that God has created and redeemed in Christ. The most fundamental attitude of the Christian in face of the divine self-giving to sinners must be gratitude. The Christian moral life, like the spiritual life, is authentically rooted in the thankful response of men and women who have heard and believed the Good News. Every moment and movement of prayer is a graced and grateful (if only implicit) human response to the divine gift of relationship offered to the Christian; every morally good action is a grateful response to the good poured out on the individual and on all of creation. It is in this context that we can see that a variety of stances in prayer as response to God can impact the decision-making of Christians by impacting them as decision-makers.

(1) *Prayer as grateful response to God* opens Christian men and women to the giftedness of their lives, of their relationships, and of their world. Prayer of thanksgiving enriches the motivations, affections, and other attitudes with which the Christian approaches moments of decision. When Christians are aware of the giftedness of their own lives, they are less prone to attitudes such as selfishness, jealousy, and impatience in their decisions. Furthermore, they can more readily recognize the giftedness of other persons involved in situations of choice. As we have had cause to note in earlier chapters, Enda McDonagh suggests that the most fundamental human experience of moral obligation— the most basic reason that human persons feel that they *ought* to do anything—is the experience of other persons as gift, as unique and irreplaceable values in themselves. It is from the experience of the immeasurable value of other persons that we experience a "call" to respond in particular ways.[4] The value of the other person creates a natural human response of respect and reverence, not only in attitude but also in action.

Christian faith teaches that all persons are created in the image of God, are redeemed by Christ, and thus are brothers and sisters of one another. This distinctive perspective certainly highlights the intuitive experience of other persons as gift. But it is precisely grateful prayer—whether the attitude of thankfulness in personal prayer or the grateful common prayer of the liturgy—that further enables us to see the other as gift. Gratitude, therefore, makes our decision-making more generous, more other-directed, more selfless. It gives the Christian a clearer vision of the persons and values at stake in the midst of the actual situation. Prayer as grateful response to God, then, impacts moral decision-making by enabling Christians to see the true and authentic value of persons in every situation of choice.

(2) *Prayer as a recommitment of one's fundamental "yes" to God,* another stance or attitude in prayer, represents the depth of the Christian's response to God. The divine love and life itself have been offered definitively to sinful humanity in Jesus Christ. What response can the human person make to such an incredible gift other than a total giving of self in return—not only in individual actions (no matter how heroic) nor in individual moments of prayer (no matter how sublime)? The stance of prayer in which Christians strive to give a total and fundamental "yes" to God has tremendous impact on their subsequent decisions, since the prayer of commitment to God at its deepest level sets the direction of every decision to be made in the future. Once one has said "yes" to God with all of the commitment of which one is presently capable, then one's moral life and moral decisions become opportunities to integrate every desire, every choice, every action into one's fundamental life commitment to God.

Thus, in the moment of decision, the person of prayer seeks to make the choice that can best be conformed to and integrated with his or her most basic fundamental option for God. Some choices and actions are seen to be immediately incompatible with such a commitment; others are seen to be conducive and authentic to it. In many cases, of course, the appropriateness of the action to one's fundamental commitment will not be immediately clear; but the more the person enters into and reaffirms that deep level of commitment to God in prayer, the more the person's intuitive sense of authenticity will be a reliable element in making a moral judgment.

(3) *Prayer as surrender to God* gives shape to the "yes" spoken to God after the model of Jesus in the garden of Gethsemane. Just

as Jesus said "Not my will but yours be done" (Lk 22:42), so too the Christian in the prayer of surrender commits himself or herself to seek God's will rather than one's own. Christians become anxious to carry out the divine will even in the most difficult situations. Prayer as surrender frees the person from selfishness at the moment of decision. Human freedom is further released from the enslavement of one's own selfish will and desires and habits. Abandonment to God's will makes the person of prayer docile to promptings of the Spirit in making good decisions and frees one to carry out the divine will in every situation. The person who in prayer seeks to surrender to God's will can more easily and faithfully seek out and discover that will in the situation of choice even if its fulfillment entails difficulty or runs contrary to one's immediate desires.

(4) *Prayer as a loving transcendence of self* is already suggested by the stance of surrender. In fact, to love always involves transcending self—to go beyond oneself for the sake of another. To be converted is to transcend one's present worldview, one's present priorities, one's current self-identity. In prayer, Christians transcend self in order to give their lives to God. In doing so, they prepare, train, and condition themselves to transcend self at the moment of decision. In situations of choice, people of prayer are better able to transcend their own "mere" satisfactions for the sake of authentic values and to transcend their own needs for the authentic needs of others, because their attitude in prayer has already disposed them to authentic selflessness. Prayer, therefore, empowers the living out of moral and affective conversion.

(5) *Prayer as an attentive listening to God*, yet another stance of prayer as response, disposes Christians to hear the voice of God speaking in the depths of their hearts. Listening prayer creates a human spirit attentive to God's promptings and direction. At the moment of choice persons of prayer hear a voice directing them that is not foreign or strange but familiar and trustworthy—like the sheep recognize the voice of their own shepherd (Jn 10:3–5). This divine voice speaks in the depths of one's heart giving guidance and encouragement to the process of decision-making. The "discernment of spirits" has been understood in the Catholic

spiritual tradition as the effort to discriminate between the various "voices" that speak to the Christian—whether of God, of evil spirits, or of the sometimes mysterious desires of one's own heart. The person who has become disposed to listen and to recognize the divine voice in prayer will more readily hear and recognize that voice in the moment of choice.

The person with a prayerful spirit of attentive openness is more docile to the Spirit's guidance in the process of decision-making. In such a person, the Spirit is able to bring greater light to bear on important values at stake and on the particular needs of the individual people involved in the situation of choice. The affective response of the person of listening prayer to relevant values and needs can be made more acute by the Spirit's movement. The person of prayer remains free, but the Spirit is able to work with natural human capacities and processes of choice to enable a decision more in line with the divine will.

(6) *Prayer as asking of God* disposes Christians to see their complete dependence on God—a dependence that does not create fear or resentment but even greater trust and gratitude. Christians who are familiar with raising petitions to God in trust are less disposed to trust in self or to decide in a way that suggests a complete autonomy from God and the workings of grace. In their acceptance of their own dependence on God, they can be more disposed to attend to the needs of other persons. Furthermore, since Christ has promised that whatever is asked in his name will be heard, the Christian can be confident that the prayer for guidance in times of decision will not go unanswered. Such a Christian asks freely for divine guidance in choosing, fully hoping that the prayer will not go unheeded and thus will be expectant, open, and trusting of the guidance offered.

(7) *Prayer as repentance* is always a response to the mercy of God already being offered. Repentance draws the person of prayer away from the selfishness of sin. It disposes the Christian to forgive others since he or she experiences the complete gratuity of God's forgiveness. The Christian, therefore, attends to the decision with greater freedom from anger or bitterness toward others. Prayer of repentance opens the eyes of Christians to their former blindness and further frees them to transcend themselves

in love, to surrender themselves more completely to God. A repentant stance in prayer, therefore, predisposes the person to see the situation of choice in new, selfless and authentic ways. To discover God's forgiveness anew in prayer leads the Christian to an even deeper sense of gratitude and thus to a more invigorated life of grateful response to God.

Prayer as Communion

Christian prayer always has the character of a response to God—whether in particular moments of prayer and decision or in the broad direction of the Christian life itself. But this prayerful response always occurs within the context of a relationship with God. Prayer builds one's relationship with God but also fundamentally presupposes it. God invites men and women into divine friendship, into the divine life itself. This communion with God is ultimately a future goal but it is also a present reality most especially because of the presence of Christ working through the Spirit. Prayer is always a privileged encounter within the context of one's friendship with God; it is always an experience of communion with God—distinctively, of course, for the contemplative but even for the beginner in prayer. It is in the context of prayer as communion—and the various stances of prayer as communion—that we can see further how prayer impacts the moral decision-making of Christians by influencing what the Christian brings to every situation.

(1) *Prayer as a developing friendship with God* attunes the Christian to the will of God just as the friendship between persons gives them a familiarity with the ways of one another. Friends come to know one another over time in such a way that they can anticipate the desires and preferences and priorities of their friend. Prayer as an ongoing relationship with God yields a "connatural" knowledge of the will of God—that is, a knowledge "born of love" that is not a conceptual, logical knowledge but a real knowledge nonetheless. This is perhaps especially true of prayer that builds one's relationship with God in Christ through meditation on scripture. Prayer as an essential aspect of the Christian's ongoing friendship with God gives the person a

unique insight into God's will in situations of choice. The Christian comes to an intuitive knowledge of what God would want based on their developing intimacy in prayer.

(2) *Prayer as a deep communion with God* draws the Christian into the life of the triune God itself, and to commune with the God who is love is to be challenged to love in every situation. The Christian life is not only a friendship with God but a developing union with God. The person of deep and authentic prayer draws ever closer to God. As this communion grows stronger in the Christian, the Christian comes to see with God's eyes, to love with God's love, to will what God wills in every situation—in short, to be conformed to God in Christ. In the effort to make decisions, the Christian appropriately asks God for special assistance in this particular situation; but more fundamentally it is prayer as communion with God that disposes the Christian to act according to the divine will, because one's spirit has already communed with the Spirit of God.

(3) *Prayer as entering more deeply into oneself* is an inevitable aspect of any deep prayer, since in prayer, one discovers the Spirit of God at work at the deepest core of one's being where the divine Spirit speaks to the spirit of the human person. Prayer, then, draws the person to the "heart" where the Christian has said the fundamental "yes" to God. In the moment of choice, the person of prayer is more fully in contact with his or her authentic self and also more aware of the sin that can blind one to the authentic good. It is easier, then, to make a good choice because the prayerful person has a greater sense of the "fittingness" of certain actions to one's own integrity as a human person and as person with a fundamental commitment to God.

Entering more deeply into oneself in prayer also forms the Christian as a decision-maker in a more "negative" way. Drawing close to God's illuminating presence reveals one's sins and the hidden roots of sin—just as a strong light reveals the flaws in an object previously shrouded in shadow. In the light of God's merciful love, the revelation of one's darkness leads not to despair but to a greater gratitude and humility. To come to a greater awareness of one's personal tendencies to sin can make the Christian more self-critical about his or her hidden motives in the decisions to be made. It can give the Christian new resolve to eradicate the roots of sin and to live and decide instead in greater consistency with one's fundamental life commitment.

(4) *Prayer as identifying oneself with God in Christ* flows obviously from communion with God. To understand oneself in reference to God is to make the divine priorities my own. To discover in the witness of Jesus, for example, God's special concern for the marginalized and for the poor becomes an aspect of the Christian's self-understanding and so necessarily part of his or her decisions. In prayer the Christian reaffirms his or her identity as a disciple of Jesus and thereby reaffirms the baptismal commitment to live a life worthy of the gospel. Participation in the liturgy plays an important role in forming and reaffirming the Christian identity, as we have seen.

In prayer, Christians come to understand themselves not only as servants, followers and disciples but as children of God—sons and daughters by adoption. Further, they come to see themselves as "participants in the divine nature" (2 Pet 1:4). Chapter 4 has described how the patristic and the Eastern Christian tradition speaks of "deification" *(theosis)* as the goal and reality of Christian life: Christians are called to become divine by participation in the life of the Trinity. To encounter this awesome gift and reality in prayer is to be challenged to live every day and indeed every moment as a true child of God and as an authentic participant in the divine nature of the loving God. Every decision becomes an invitation to actualize this deified existence through choices that are in line with the divine life as this has been revealed in Jesus and is being continually revealed in the life of the Spirit.

(5) *Prayer as communion with others in God* is an essential—if not always apparent—aspect of communion with God since God is the creator and redeemer, the ground of all life, and the parent of all men and women. Prayer can certainly be "private" in the sense of "personal" but it can never be individualistic, cut off from other people. Prayer—especially but not exclusively prayer for and with others—leads Christians to understand themselves as necessarily related to others and thus as necessarily concerned for them.

Authentic prayer leads Christians to seek out authentic

human relationships. As we saw in chapter 5, the search for "right relationships" is a foundation of justice, and it is a presupposition of love. Prayer as communion with others in God challenges the Christian to act justly in every situation of choice and to act so that any other people touched by one's decision may be drawn into more healthy and more authentically human relationships. This is true not only at the interpersonal level but also at the structural level where political, economic and cultural institutions can benefit or hinder authentic relationships between and among people of different races, gender, and class.

(6) *Prayer as communing with nature* also flows necessarily from communion with God since God is the creator and sustainer of the whole created order. Authentic prayer leads the Christian to value all of creation as signs of the presence and love of its creator. While the Christian's communion with nature may be most intensely experienced while in the midst of natural beauty, all authentic communion with God implicitly draws one to a new reverence for creation. In the moment of decision, therefore, the Christian is challenged to decide so as to respect and reverence the good of the natural order, of the environment.

Some Final Reflections

Prayer impacts the Christian as a moral decision-maker in significant ways. But while prayer is utterly essential to good Christian decision-making, it cannot and should not replace rational reflection, careful analyses, and the "application" of relevant rules and norms. Reliance on such common human resources is especially vital for those who are beginners in prayer—that is, for the vast majority of Christians who have not yet attained the integrity of both sustained virtue and of true holiness in which the person's desires, loves, words, thoughts, actions, decisions, and prayers have become fully integrated into their relationship with God. Prayer, then, is necessary to good decision-making but alone is not sufficient for it. (An exception might be those individuals who have grown so close to God, so disposed to do good, and so docile to the promptings of the Spirit, that they can have a reliable intuition of the good without the use of other means.)

To suggest that prayer is essential to good decisions, therefore, is not to suggest that prayer becomes the Christian's *only* basis for moral choices—independent of the light that God also offers through human reason, established laws, and the guidance of the church. It is to suggest, however, that without prayer these other essential means of making good decisions are also not sufficient. In fact, authentic prayer draws the Christian to discover and to value every means that God uses to guide men and women to the good. The person of authentic prayer becomes more—not less—attentive to reason, to laws, and to the wisdom of the church, since each is another path to know God's will more completely and therefore allows the Christian to respond to God more authentically. At the same time, prayer may reveal to Christians that God is calling them to *more* than the demands of reason and of laws, and to even more than what church teaching requires of them.

To say that prayer is essential to good decision-making is also not to suggest that non-Christians, or at least people who do not pray, cannot make good choices. Practical experience makes clear that people who do not pray, in fact, can and do regularly make good choices. There are situations in which human reason, the rules that flow from it, and the application of these rules in concrete situations are sufficient for good decisions. And so, it cannot be argued that prayer is "essential" in the sense of "always required for every situation"; but prayer *is* "essential" for the *consistency* of good decisions over time in the face of complex and conflicted situations and in the presence of sin both personal and social. Reason, in order to be truly and consistently reliable, must be "informed by faith."

Prayer impacts decision-making by changing the person who prays, the person who decides. When truly prayerful Christians come to choose a course of action, they come with important tools and dispositions to make a good choice. Prayer changes the Christian's relationship with God, self, other persons, and the world after the model and according to the priorities of the God who invites men and women into communion in Christ. Prayer thus transforms the person who decides, and so prayer transforms the moral decisions of those who pray.

8

DECISION-MAKING AS DISCERNMENT

The word "discernment" for the average Catholic often implies the effort to decide about a vocation to the priesthood or to professed religious life. Young men and women "discern" a possible call from God to a life of ministry. This decision-making of the Christian about a vocation clearly involves the effort to come to understand God's will for a particular person in a particular situation. But the word "discernment" can also be used appropriately of the other decisions in the Christian's life—that is, of the moral decisions that Christians make every day. Christians are called to "discern" God's will in the choices that face them in their personal lives, in their relationships, in their workplaces, and in their political choices. The moral decision-making of Christians is not primarily a matter of obeying rules, applying norms, and rational analyses that only in some more remote way reflect God's will; rather the Christian seeks to discover God's will in every situation. Norms, laws and logical analyses play an important role in discovering God's will but they by no means exhaust the challenge of discernment in Christian moral decision-making.

In the previous chapter, we looked at how a life of prayer forms the Christian as a decision-maker. In the present chapter, we will argue that the moral decisions of Christians can never be separated from the effort to discern and to carry out God's will for the individual person in the present circumstances. God's loving will for the individual is not restricted to some broad, general plan for the individual's life but is to be discovered in every situation of choice. Every decision is an opportunity and an invitation to respond to the God who is always present, offering more abundant life. The moral decision-making of Christians, then, necessarily involves discernment: the effort to discover and to carry out God's will for each individual as it is revealed in the rules and laws taught by the community, in the particularities of the concrete situation itself, and in the response "of the heart" where the spirit of the Christian encounters the Spirit of God. Moral decision-making and "spiritual discernment" can no more be separated than can the Christian's moral life be separated from his or her spiritual life.

The present effort to demonstrate that the moral decision-making of Christians is a form of discernment will proceed in the following steps: (1) A brief overview of some recent literature on discernment will provide the overall context for our discussion. (2) A review of the rule-based method of making moral choices current before the Second Vatican Council will explicate the task that lies ahead for a more adequate understanding of Christian decision-making. (3) An examination of the Thomistic perspective on the role of the virtues and gifts of the Holy Spirit in actual situations of choice will offer some suggestions for a broader and more adequate view of Christian moral reflection in concrete situations. (4) A discussion of some contemporary trends in moral theology will suggest some advances in current theological reflection on making decisions. (5) We will then draw together the foregoing discussion into a more constructive statement about Christian moral decision-making as the "prudential discernment" of God's will.

Meanings of Discernment

"Discernment of spirits" has been a frequent subject in the literature of Christian spirituality.[1] Certainly because discernment holds such an important place in Ignatius Loyola's *Spiritual Exercises*, Jesuits in particular have devoted themselves to scholarly study of this important topic.[2] Several more popular studies of discernment have expanded on the Ignatian reflections and suggested some broader uses of the traditional wisdom about discernment.[3] Several recent works on spiritual direction have discussed the importance of understanding discernment in the spiritual direction relationship.[4]

Discernment of spirits is usually described as the effort to discriminate between the various inner movements, "voices," or "spirits" that arise from within as we strive to discover God's will for us in particular situations. Classical treatments have suggested that these spirits can be the Spirit of God, evil spirits, or the sometimes mysterious movements of the human heart itself. In a brief, more popular description, Thomas Green calls discernment "the art of finding God's will in the concrete life situations which confront us."[5] Several points need to be clarified from the foregoing statements.

Jules Toner makes an important distinction in Ignatius' thought between the "discernment of spirits" and the "discernment of God's will."[6] The discernment of spirits allows Christians to discriminate between the various spirits at work within them, but this does not yet yield knowledge of God's will. Actual discernment of God's will in particular situations of choice requires additional factors such as consideration of options, likely consequences, and previous experience in similar circumstances. Discerning God's will goes beyond the "discernment of spirits" then, strictly speaking. While a good deal of the literature dealing with discernment does not make this distinction precisely, it is well to keep it in mind. Discernment in moral decision-making is an attempt to discover God's will for a particular agent in a concrete historical situation. "Discernment of spirits" may be an important aspect of making sound decisions, as the person tries to attain some clarity about the various "voices" within (whether actual spirits, deeply felt urges, or compulsions), but moral decision-making and moral discernment remain broader.

It is clear from the literature on discernment that the authentic discovery of God's will is not possible without an adequate foundation in the person who wishes to discern. This foundation includes a number of interrelated elements.[7] The person must be committed to growing in his or her relationship with God. This is the context in which the person develops a life of prayer which is utterly essential to authentic discernment since, as the subtitle of Thomas Green's book suggests, discernment is "where prayer and action meet." A growing friendship with God and a life of prayer yield a certain "knowledge" of God and of the divine ways "born of love"—that is, a "connatural" knowledge. The person who hopes to discern must possess a true desire, openness, and commitment to do what God wills as the divine will begins to be revealed. This openness requires a trust that God does, in fact, reveal the divine will and that God's will is always loving. The openness for discernment also requires an interior freedom ("indifference," "detachment," "purity of heart") from disordered desire and attachments that can prevent the discerner from hearing and/or carrying out God's will.

More recently, there have been several important studies of "moral discernment"—that is, of discerning God's will in the context of concrete moral decision-making.[8] The main directions of these studies will be discussed below. It is important at present to see that the tradition of discernment in general presupposes that God's will is, in fact, directed to particular persons in concrete situations and that the challenge of discerning the divine will in the lived experience of Christians is not rare or exceptional.[9] Indeed it is the thesis of the present chapter that authentic Christian moral decision-making must always have the character of discerning the divine will in the here and now.

Rule-Based Moral Decision-Making

The Catholic moral theology current immediately before the Second Vatican Council saw little place for discernment in the moral life of Christians. One's moral obligation in particular situations was determined largely by reference to established rules. When a Christian came to a situation of choice, the first questions to be asked were, "What is my duty?" and "What is the relevant rule that will make my duty clear?" This rule-based view of decision-making is called a "deontological" model as opposed to a goal-based or "teleological" model whose first question in a situation of choice is, "What is the goal to be pursued?"[10]

Moral decision-making, then, was understood by this older approach to be the application of moral norms to concrete situations or as the deduction of concrete moral obligations from universal norms. The process of deciding, then, could be laid out almost like a syllogism with the universal moral norm as the major premise and an analysis of the concrete situation in which the norm was to be applied as the minor premise. Moral decision-making in this perspective is basically the conclusion reached by the logical reasoning through this syllogistic process.

The distinctively Christian bases for decision in this rule-based model are present but not immediately apparent. The acceptance of and fidelity to one's duty in following established norms and laws can be understood as an important part of one's broader religious purpose—that is, attaining communion with God who is the ultimate source of these moral norms. This is, in fact, the theological foundation of Catholic natural law theory: the presupposition that the natural law revealed the divine law, God's will. To follow the rules, then, would be an implicit following of God's will. These norms or laws often receive further certainty of manifesting God's will through the support of scriptural warrants or through official explication by the church's magisterium with its special charism of teaching. In deducing one's particular moral duty in the concrete situation from universal norms, then, the Christian had reason to believe that he or she was accomplishing or at least not violating God's will through the decisions reached.

While this method of decision-making seems to offer an attractive clarity and simplicity, several deficiencies are readily apparent. There are, of course, many situations in which there are no clear rules or in which it is not clear how relevant rules might apply. Similarly, the deductive, rule-based method does not seem to give sufficient attention to the unique qualities present in every concrete historical situation with wide possible variables in the persons involved and in the surrounding circumstances of time and place. Further, this method seems to suggest that "blind" obedience to rules can be held up as a virtue, a notion that runs contrary to a richer sense of Christian moral living as a response to other persons and to God with adult freedom and responsibility.

In fact, the rule-based method of decision-making seems to imply an inadequate view of the Christian moral life as primarily involving obedience to laws. There is no doubt that laws hold an important place in the moral life, but the way of Christian discipleship as expressed in the scriptures seems to suggest a much broader and richer view of Christian living. It would be difficult to see the relevance of discernment in the context of this rule-based approach to moral decision-making. Furthermore, prayer might serve at best as a useful introduction to or confirmation of the rational, deductive process of making decisions, but prayer does not seem integral to these choices.[11]

Reclaiming Thomistic Perspectives

The deductive, rule-based approach to moral decision-making claimed a foundation in the moral theology of St. Thomas, and Aquinas certainly discusses the natural law and the rational elements in the moral acts of the human person. As many contemporary studies of the moral theology of St. Thomas emphasize, however, Aquinas was far more concerned with virtues than with law in the Christian life.[12] His attention to rational elements in moral acts does not exclude other non-rational elements in decision-making. Furthermore, Aquinas sees the moral life within the context of the dynamism of the Christian life moving toward God, with the assistance of the Holy Spirit, particularly through the infused virtues and the gifts of the Holy Spirit. A sound moral choice could not be reduced, then, to the application of norms to concrete situations. A review of Thomistic thought will demonstrate that part of our task in coming to understand Christian decision-making as discernment is, in fact, a task of reclaiming important elements of our tradition.

St. Thomas' concern for discernment in the moral life is found in the context of his discussion of the virtue of prudence—especially as directed and perfected by grace.[13] For St. Thomas, good moral decision-making is certainly not relativistic; it does entail attention to the objective good, to established norms. But making good decisions is not simply a matter of applying norms to concrete situations; it is not just a matter of a rational, logical process. Making good decisions for the Christian requires the appropriation of virtue, the formation of character, which becomes the internal "context" from which the Christian understands the situation, decides, and acts. Ultimately, truly good decisions require grace, the working of the Spirit in the mind and the heart of the Christian in the act of deciding in particular cases.

For Aquinas, virtues—habitual dispositions—are central to the Christian moral life. There are a number of moral virtues which can all be understood as related to the four basic "cardinal" virtues of prudence, justice, temperance, and fortitude. Prudence, in particular, guides these other virtues since it is the habitual disposition to act well (*ST* II-II, q.47).[14] It is prudence that enables the person to come to an understanding of the circumstances of the situation of choice and to know what action is morally appropriate to these particular realities. Principles and norms play an important role in prudential decision-making, since it is a function of prudence to apply relevant norms to concrete situations. Prudence goes further, however, together with a related virtue that St. Thomas calls *gnome*, in reaching decisions in those cases where rules do not exist or do not apply to particular circumstances (*ST* II-II, q.51, a.4). It is in this sense that we can speak of the operation of prudence in good decision-making as "prudential discernment."

The moral virtues, including prudence, are "acquired" in the sense that they are good habits built up over time by consistently good moral actions—in the case of prudence, by acting prudently. But there is also an important sense in which the virtues are "infused"—given by God with grace (*ST* I-II, q.63). When God indwells the Christian's life in grace, God infuses the theological virtues of faith, hope and charity together with infused moral virtues to "match" those virtues acquired through human effort. The *infused* moral virtues—such as the *infused* virtue of prudence—further perfect the operation of the intellect and will in moral action. Reason is "informed by faith"—enabled and empowered by grace in moral decisions and actions through the graced operation of prudential moral discernment. The infusion of virtue, for Aquinas, does not remove or eliminate the need for human effort but rather empowers and directs those efforts. As Bernard Häring says of infused virtue:

> Our doctrine on the infused moral virtues clearly reveals the source and basis and also the end and goal of Christian virtue: the foundation and source is the Holy Spirit with His transforming and renovating grace; [the] end and goal are Christ and the Father, the imitation of the spirit of Christ through the force of His Spirit.[15]

The infused virtue of prudence for St. Thomas, then, represents the assistance of grace in coming to good moral decisions.

Furthermore, all of the virtues in the grace-filled Christian are further directed and empowered by the infused theological virtue of charity. Charity, defined by St. Thomas as friendship with God (*ST* II-II, q.23, a.1), directs all of the other virtues toward attaining communion with God. Charity becomes the "form" of the virtues (*ST* I-II, q.65, a. 3; II-II, q.23, a.8)—we might say that our love of God seeks to integrate every other disposition or action into this fundamental desire for, love of, choice for God. Charity, in turn, "flows over from the will to the intellect and in doing so becomes wisdom, contributing its own orientation and discernment to all the other virtues and qualities which man possesses."[16] Charity functions, therefore, to perfect our moral decision-making by disposing us to direct—to integrate—all of our decisions and actions into our fundamental, developing friendship with God.

Demonstrating even further his belief in the Christian moral life as a life of the Spirit, St. Thomas maintains that God infuses the Christian with the gifts of the Holy Spirit: understanding, knowledge, wisdom, counsel (right judgment), piety, fortitude, and fear of the Lord (*ST* I-II, q.68).[17] These gifts together make the Christian open to, docile to, the promptings of the Holy Spirit. They perfect the virtues—no longer through the use of reason (even reason informed by faith) but by the inspiration and direction of the Spirit (*ST* I-II, q.68, aa.1,2). In doing so, the gifts do not operate contrary to natural human capacities but in conjunction with them. Wisdom, as we have seen, perfects charity in that it makes the Christian attuned to the things of God and to those things which are pleasing to God even in concrete matters of choice (*ST* II-II, q.45). Wisdom, therefore, has a vital place in helping the Christian to decide in a manner that will be in accord with God's will. In a similar way, the gift of counsel perfects the virtue of prudence, guiding the Christian to choose according to the inspiration of the Holy Spirit in a manner not contrary to reason and to norms but beyond them (*ST* II-II, q.52, aa.1,2).

Christian decision-making, then, cannot be reduced to applying norms to particular situations; and the prudential discernment that constitutes a more adequate view of Christian choosing is not simply a function of prudence in the sense of a naturally acquired skill or virtue to decide well (although it includes this). Rather, the prudential discernment of Christians is Spirit-guided, Spirit-inspired, Spirit-empowered. The Spirit of God helps the Christian to decide in the concrete situation in a manner that will be pleasing to God, that can be integrated with one's developing friendship with God, and that can draw one closer to God. Thus, Christian prudential discernment, decision-making, is not only *not* simply a matter of applying norms to concrete situations, it is *not even* a matter of the perfection of some human capacity. It is discernment aided by the Holy Spirit working with and through human capacities—and sometimes beyond them—ultimately aimed at communion with God.

The discussion of virtues and gifts as infused with grace is not meant to suggest some complete package given to the Christian—as if with this infusion, the Christian is able to live a perfect moral life and to make perfect moral decisions. The fact of sin and human limit makes this immediate and complete transformation virtually impossible. In fact, such development of virtues, such integration of one's dispositions into one's developing friendship with God in charity, and such growth in docility to the promptings of the Spirit take a lifetime of effort and of openness to God. Although virtues and gifts are infused, they can and must become more effective in the Christian's life as one's friendship with God—one's charity—grows. And so it is in the lived experience of sincere Christians who discover that growth in virtue, growth in charity, growth in holiness is the task of a lifetime.

Contemporary Perspectives on Decision-Making

In addition to the intrinsic problems with an exclusive focus on norms and laws in the moral decision-making of Christians, and together with the Thomistic tradition itself, a number of contemporary trends in Catholic moral theology suggest a different and more adequate perspective on the moral choices of Christians. Attending to these trends will allow us to formulate a more constructive alternative to the deductive, rule-based model of decision-making.

A more Christocentric and biblically based moral theology suggests that the Christian moral life cannot be adequately understood merely as obedience to laws. The Christian life is a life of discipleship in which the Christian strives to make a total response to the God who has so generously offered life, friendship, and communion in Christ Jesus. Just as the self-giving love of God is most perfectly manifest in Jesus, so too the shape of the authentic human response to God is made manifest in Jesus. The precise shape of this response in the concrete situations and decisions of life, however, can be reduced neither to a simple imitation of Christ nor to a mere obedience to norms and laws. In this broader and more holistic view of the Christian moral life, discerning God's will through the working of the Holy Spirit can take on a more important place.

In light of the understanding of the moral life as a relationship between God and humanity and as the response of human persons to God's self-offering, some Christian ethicists are suggesting that the traditional deontological (rule- or duty-based) and even the teleological (goal-based) views of the moral life are no longer adequate. Instead, they recommend a "relationality-responsibility" view of the Christian life.[18] In this newer perspective, the effort to determine one's concrete moral duty does not begin with the question, "What is my duty?" (deontology) nor, "What is my goal?" (teleology) but with the question,"What is God enabling and requiring me to do in the present moment?" The answer to this question requires discernment.

Another trend in contemporary moral theology that suggests a more adequate view of Christian decision-making is a renewed understanding and emphasis on personal conscience and human freedom.[19] The Second Vatican Council reiterates and furthers the traditional Catholic emphasis on the morally binding nature of the well-formed conscience. The human conscience represents the very dignity of the human person and is "the most secret core and sanctuary" of the human person in which the voice of God echoes.[20] Making free choices based on an authentic and well-formed conscience is at the heart of the moral life.

The prime importance of conscience in no way suggests a moral relativism in which an action is right simply because I "sincerely" believe it to be; rather, the authentic conscience guides the human person within the context of the objective good."[21] The Catholic emphasis on conscience, then, is by no means antinomian— nor, however, can the Christian moral life be reduced to obeying rules or deducing concrete moral obligations from universal norms. The more holistic contemporary view of conscience suggests a view of the Christian moral life and moral decision-making in which human persons are understood to be striving to respond to God in concrete situations with a mature and critical freedom. From this perspective, blind and uncritical obedience is not only *not* a virtue; it is a vice.

Criticism of the deductive, rule-based model of decision-making, together with a broader understanding of the functioning of conscience, led Karl Rahner to a view of concrete "existential" decision-making in which discernment plays an important part.[22] Rahner argues that God directs the divine will to individuals not only through universal norms but also in their concrete situations. For this reason, moral decision-making must be more than simply deducing one's moral obligation from universal norms in the concrete situation:

> It would be absurd for a God-regulated, theological morality
> to think that God's binding will could only be directed to the
> human action in so far as the latter is simply a realization of

the universal norm and of a universal nature. If the creative
will of God is directly and unambiguously directed to the
concrete and the individual, then surely this is not merely in
so far as this individual reality is the realization of a case of
the universal—rather it is directed to the concrete as such, as
it really is—to the concrete in its positive, and particularly its
substantial, material uniqueness.[23]

Conscience, for Rahner, in turn, has a double function: in some
situations, to apply general norms to concrete situations but also,
in other situations, to discover in the concrete situation God's
unique call to the individual.[24] In the latter case, conscience
functions through the process of discernment to discover the
response which most "fits" with the individual's fundamental
commitment, option, for God.

Another contemporary trend in Catholic moral theology that
directs it away from a deductive, rule-based approach to decision-
making is its greater attention to non-rational (that is not to say
*ir*rational) elements in moral choice. The duty-based perspective
implied that the more one could abstract from the affective
dimensions of a situation, the more rational and thus the better
decision one could make. Without in any way denying the
importance of rational analysis, contemporary Catholic moral
theology is attending to the affective and imaginative dimensions
of the moral life. Moral theologian Philip Keane, for example, has
demonstrated the importance of the moral imagination in a
renewed Catholic moral theology.[25]

Nowhere is this non-rational approach more evident,
however, than in the contemporary emphasis on the distinctively
Christian character as the foundation from which all moral
decision-making flows.[26] In sum, a distinctively Christian moral
character is appropriated through the internalizing of the images,
stories, and symbols of the Christian community—most
especially those associated with Jesus. Thus the Christian brings
to every situation of choice distinctively Christian perspectives,
dispositions, affections, and intentions which necessarily impact
those decisions. As we have seen in the preceding section, the
emphasis on virtue and character is consistent with the moral

theology of St. Thomas and results in an approach to moral discernment grounded in the distinctively Christian character.

Emphasis on this context of Christian decision-making leads Protestant ethicist James Gustafson to suggest the importance of moral discernment.[27] This perspective has been further highlighted by William Spohn in reaction to the deductive model of decision-making as well as to Rahner's alternative perspective.[28] For Gustafson, moral decision-making is the effort to discern what God enables and requires the Christian to do in the concrete situation. This moral discernment involves at least three common elements: (1) a "reading" of the situation; (2) the moral agent himself or herself, his or her character—that is, persistent moral dispositions, moral sensitivities, and basic convictions; and (3) the beliefs, rules and principles that inform the discernment and the rational reflection about how these function in the concrete situation.

For Gustafson, the discernment itself involves both rational and affective aspects of the person including a "moral sensitivity" that contributes an important intuitive element to decision-making. The Christian faith impacts moral discernment at every level, since faith informs the way in which the agent understands self and the world around him or her, and what the agent values, intends, and desires. Faith gives the Christian a unique perspective for discerning what God enables and requires. Since faith and character are formed within community, discernment must occur within the context of the Christian community.

William Spohn argues that in addition to the "reasoning head" that has generally been the focus of attention in the Catholic approach to decision-making, authentic Christian choices must also involve discernment through a "reasoning heart." The discerning heart makes affective judgments in concrete situations based on the person's faith and character. The authenticity of Christian discernment is tested against the self-understanding of the agent in light of the story of Jesus which makes normative claims on the way persons should be. It is also tested against the normative affections modelled by Jesus—affections which become rooted in the Christian's character and which offer intuitions of appropriate behavior. Spohn summarizes:

> Christian discernment brings to light rich elements in moral decision-making. Judgments of affectivity legitimately ground some moral decisions through discriminating functions of memory and imagination. These judgments are evaluated not by formal logic but by aesthetic criteria: by the sense of self, the evaluation of events through biblical symbols, and the correlation between certain ways of acting and the configuration of Christian affections.[29]

The contemporary trends in Catholic moral theology discussed in the present section cohere with the more focused contemporary studies of the basic human decision-making process. These studies emphasize the importance of taking into account more diverse elements in the process of making moral decisions. One of the most prominent leaders in this broadening of the decision-making process has been Daniel Maguire whose well-received 1978 work, *The Moral Choice*[30] has been refined in his 1991 collaborative work with A. Nicholas Fargnoli, *On Moral Grounds*.[31] Maguire and Fargnoli argue that the "foundational moral experience" from which all obligations arise is the affective response to the value of persons.[32] All authentic human values are related to this most basic human value of human persons. Ethics, then, is the "art/science that seeks to bring sensitivity and method to the discernment of moral values."[33] Moral decision-making involves the effort to discover (discern) the best way to realize authentic values in the concrete situation.

The model for decision-making suggested by Maguire and Fargnoli involves two phases. The *questioning* phase seeks to reveal the complex reality present in the situation of choice through a number of "reality revealing questions" (i.e., what? why? how? who? when? where? foreseeable effects? viable options?). No human action, they argue, can be judged outside the context of its actual circumstances. The *evaluating* phase involves the effort to examine and judge the circumstances revealed in the first phase through a number of different lenses: creative imagination, affectivity, reasoned analysis, authority, principles, individual and group experience, and tragedy and comedy. It is from such careful analysis and broad evaluation of the circumstances of choice that the individual can hope to make the decision which best secures the values at stake.

The work of Maguire and Fargnoli is important to the present discussion of discernment and decision-making for a number of reasons. It certainly argues against a purely deductive, rule-based approach to decision-making. It suggests that many factors other than logical, rational analysis are needed; in fact, they maintain that affectivity, feeling, is an important kind of moral knowing in itself. Their study further suggests that discovering the values to be secured is precisely a matter of discernment, of an affective response to value. Their focus on values that serve human persons can also be the ground of a renewed understanding of the natural law, offering the foundation for the objective dimension of morality in addition to the affective dimension suggested by the emphasis on feeling, imagination, character and virtue. Both dimensions are important to the moral life and to moral decision-making, and both have been consistent elements of Catholic moral reflection.

Because Maguire and Fargnoli are not writing for an exclusively Christian audience, they do not explicitly discuss the ways that the factors in the evaluating phase can be impacted by Christian faith. Their emphasis on affective, creative and imaginative dimensions, however, suggests clear avenues for distinctively Christian interpretations of their criteria. The Christian comes to every situation of choice, not only with the capacities for rational analysis and decision shared with all of humanity, but also with distinctive perspectives that will necessarily impact one's understanding of the situation and of the moral demands that arise within it.[34] As we have seen in a previous chapter, the liturgy plays an important role in forming distinctively Christian perspectives.

Prudential Discernment and Moral Decision-Making

The foregoing summaries and analyses can now allow us to present a more constructive statement of Christian moral decision-making as a form of discernment. Perhaps most important is the necessity of understanding the decision-making of Christians within the context of the Christian life itself. Christians cannot make good choices reliably and consistently outside the context of their relationship with God in Christ through the presence of the Holy Spirit. They cannot become good and perform right actions independent of their effort to grow in their relationship with God. The moral choices of Christians, therefore, must have reference to Christ and appeal to the working of the Holy Spirit in their daily lives. Christ, as the normative expression of authentic humanity and of the authentic human response to God, must shape Christian decision-making—just as the presence of the Holy Spirit must direct and empower those decisions.

The effort to live the Christian moral life is, as the title of Dubay's study of discernment *(Authenticity)* suggests, the graced effort to be authentic at every moment to the call of God in Christ, to the status of adopted children of God, and to the invitation to an ever deeper relationship with the triune God. Discernment represents the effort of the Christian to discover the authentic response to God in the concrete situation as the expression of God's will in the present moment. Christian decision-making becomes the effort to discern the "appropriateness" or "fittingness" of moral choices in light of the tools that God provides to guide the authentic response of Christians to the divine initiative.

A discerning judgment—that is, the recognition of the call to authenticity in the present situation—clearly requires a sound, critical understanding of the situation itself. What God is asking of me—what my relationship with God is demanding of me— in the present situation cannot become clear without an understanding of the circumstances themselves. The "reality revealing" questions offered by Maguire and Fargnoli in the "questioning" phase of decision-making would be extremely useful in this situational analysis.

What is the appropriate, the authentic, response in the concrete situation as the individual has come to understand it? How can his or her concrete moral obligation be discerned in the situation? Several interrelated elements can be suggested against which Christians can judge the "appropriateness," the authenticity, of their decisions.

First, potential choices for the Christian can be judged in light of their appropriateness to the Christian story—to the normative perspectives, dispositions, affections, and intentions that are revealed in Jesus, in the scriptures, in the lives of the saints. The more that Christians internalize the Christian story, the more they will be able to grasp the authentic values in each situation and the appropriateness of their actions. Christians will have a "feel" for the right choice in light of their appropriation of the Christian story:

> The present moment fits within the story which forms the individual's character, and that story must be appropriate to the normative context of the story of Jesus for the believer. This normative context can guide discernment by suggesting the response which best "fits in."[35]

Second, the options in a situation of choice can be assessed in light of the values that serve human flourishing and the norms that seek to enshrine and protect these values. From a Catholic perspective, the objectivity of morality is grounded in the natural human tendency to values that serve human flourishing—that is, the value of persons and other values that mediate the foundational value of persons. Norms arise as communities reflect on values and devise norms and laws that serve to enshrine and to protect these values. Since authentic values flow from creation by God and can lead us to God as the source of all good, the norms that arise from the recognition of value can be an authentic way of revealing the shape of the authentic response to God in the concrete situation.

Furthermore, these values and norms—if they are authentic—are clarified and confirmed in the scriptures especially in the life and teaching of Jesus and in the tradition. To say that one can assess the appropriateness of decisions against the values that serve authentic human flourishing is to suggest that discernment seeks to assess the appropriateness of decisions in light of authentic humanity itself—modelled most perfectly in the life of Jesus. From a Catholic perspective, the official teachers of the church have the special responsibility and charism for drawing together the wisdom of the Christian community—as discovered in reflection on lived experience, in the scriptures and in tradition—into moral teaching for the church. This objective dimension of morality is not contrary to the more affective and dispositional dimensions being emphasized today but operate in conjunction with them to reveal one's concrete moral duty. The deductive, rule-based approach to moral decision-making is not inadequate because it depends on norms and laws but because it placed exclusive emphasis on this essential element in coming to know God's will to the exclusion of other important elements.

Third, Christian decision-making seeks the appropriateness of potential decisions in light of the most fundamental life commitment—that is, one's "fundamental option" for God. The Christian life is a dynamic commitment to relationship with God. The Christian's "yes" to the divine invitation to communion with God seeks to become total so that the growing Christian life seeks to integrate all of the person's dispositions and choices into the positive response to God. Moral decision-making involves the effort to integrate particular actions into one's most fundamental "choice"; or, in Thomistic terms, charity as friendship with God seeks to direct all other virtues and actions to the ultimate end which is communion with God. Is this action appropriate, authentic, to one's fundamental option? Can it be integrated with that commitment? These questions certainly require critical rational analysis in light of relevant norms, but they cannot bypass a sense of appropriateness to the commitment being lived out at the depth of one's being, a depth which is not entirely available to my conscious and critical reflection.

Fourth, the decisions of Christians must be judged in light of their status as sons and daughters of God, brothers and sisters of Christ and of one another. To state this even more strongly, Christians must make decisions in light of being "partakers in the divine nature" (2 Pet 1:4). As we suggested in earlier chapters, the Christian life is a life of deification—of becoming divine by participation in the triune life of God in Christ by the power of the Holy Spirit. Christian decision-making occurs within the context of the process of deification involving a discernment *(diakrisis)* of the appropriateness of particular acts to the participation of the Christian in the divine life.[36]

Fifth, Christians must make their decisions in light of the promptings of the Holy Spirit whose voice speaks from within. The important place that St. Thomas gives to the infused virtues, to charity as the "form" of the virtues, and especially to the gifts of the Holy Spirit indicates the important place he gives to the role of the Spirit in the moral life and choices of Christians. Furthermore, Aquinas' emphasis on the essential role of prudence, acquired and infused, in concrete decision-making—especially as perfected by the operation of charity and the gifts of counsel and wisdom—demonstrates his belief in the importance of non-rational and Spirit-guided elements of Christian choosing. Good Christian decisions require, then, not only clearer thinking and better moral learning but also growth in both virtue and in holiness. Christians striving to become good moral decision-makers must grow in prayer and in their relationship with God, so that they can become accustomed to recognizing and responding to the voice of the Spirit.

All of these elements are involved in some way in good Christian decision-making. All of them clearly involve something more than deducing obligations from universal norms and rational analyses. Together they point to the broad nature of Christian decision-making as prudential discernment.

It is apparent from all of the considerations discussed above that good Christian moral decision-making is a "tall order." It requires careful reflection, critical analysis, and sustained prayer. It presupposes consistently nurtured dispositions, affections, and intentions. Obviously, authentic Christian moral discernment requires overcoming sin and disordered attachments that prevent the Christian from knowing the good, both intellectually and affectively, and from doing it. It requires a better understanding of values and the norms that enshrine them, growth in virtue, a deeper internalization of the Christian story, and growth in prayer and thus in relationship and openness to the Holy Spirit. Christian decision-making requires the Christian to become ever a better Christian, an ever more faithful disciple of Jesus.

It becomes further apparent, then, that good Christian decision-making requires the Christian community. Moral discernment is impossible to accomplish alone. Good decisions require the guidance that comes from the moral teaching of the church and the shared wisdom of the Christian community. It requires the witness, the advice and the correction that comes from other Christians. It requires the re-telling and celebration of the Christian story in the scriptures, in the liturgical calendar, in the liturgical celebration itself so that Christians may further internalize it. Good Christian decision-making requires the growth in relationship with God made possible through the sacramental life of the church—the strengthening of the fundamental life commitment of the Christian. Moral discernment, then, requires the church, and it must occur within the context of the church if it is to grow and to remain authentic.

Christian moral decision-making is a prudential discernment, rooted in the ongoing transformation of the Christian by the power of the Holy Spirit, and directed by the Spirit to discovering the good to be done in every situation. As St. Paul says: "Do not be conformed to this world, but be transformed by the renewing of your minds, so that you may discern what is the will of God—what is good and acceptable and perfect" (Rom 12:2 NRSV).

CONCLUSION
A SUMMARY STATEMENT

The Christian life is essentially a life of gratitude. Becoming a disciple of Jesus Christ involves the hearing and acceptance of the Good News that "God so loved the world that he gave his only Son, so that everyone who believes in him may not perish but may have eternal life" (Jn 3:16 NRSV). But more, the Christian comes to see that the divine love is so utterly gratuitous that it has been poured forth in Christ's death and resurrection "while we were yet sinners" (Rom 5:8). Christian life is rooted in the realization of God's loving and utterly gratuitous mercy toward sinners—and not only toward sinners in general but toward oneself as a sinner—and not just on one occasion but constantly, time and time again, irrevocably. God's merciful love begets wonder; wonder begets gratitude; and gratitude, empowered by the further working of divine love in grace, begets the Christian life.

Gratitude, for the Christian, is realized in a *life* of grateful *response*, because God's love manifests itself not only in forgiveness but in invitation. In Christ, God not only forgives, God *reconciles* humanity with himself. God's forgiveness is directed toward relationship, toward friendship. In love, God offers the divine life itself to sinful men and women. The more that Christians draw close to God in Christ, the more they come to know the love that God so generously offers to them; and the

145

more that they glimpse the incredible expanse and utter gratuity of God's love, the more that they wish to respond in gratitude and with the totality of their lives.

In the end, however, what God holds out to Christians is not simply friendship nor even "simply" the exalted status as adopted daughters and sons. God invites women and men to become participants in the divine nature itself—that is, *theosis*. Christians look forward to the day in which they will see God face-to-face and be like him:

> See what love the Father has given us, that we should be called children of God; and that is what we are. The reason that the world does not know us is that it did not know him. Beloved, we are God's children now; what we will be has not yet been revealed. What we do know is this: when he is revealed, we will be like him, for we shall see him as he is (1 Jn 3:1–2 NRSV).

Like the young children of immensely wealthy parents, Christians cannot yet fully appreciate the wonderful treasure that is held for them as their inheritance. But Christian maturity brings a greater appreciation of what God holds in store, and therefore it brings yet a further impetus for grateful response.

The experience of gratitude is the beginning of conversion. Christian conversion is the turning to God in response to God's gracious self-offering in Christ. Women and men who have even glimpsed such incredible love must be transformed by it; and, in love's illumination, they realize that the darkness of their ignorance and refusal of God's love must be scattered. The creator and redeemer and sanctifier of all offers the divine life to sinful creatures; and God's outpouring of love, as Lonergan has so vividly described, leads to an other-worldly falling in love with the God who has first loved us. Conversion, then, is the dynamic state of grateful self-transcendence in which one strives to give oneself to God. And so gratitude is the beginning of conversion, whether one becomes a disciple of Jesus by an adult decision or whether one moves from a merely nominal adherence to Christian faith to a critical appropriation of one's faith.

Conversion, as a response to the divine self-giving, seeks a *total* surrender of oneself to God in love. Every aspect of one's life and of one's relationships must be transformed so that it can be offered to God. Every encumbrance of sin—of one's personal refusal of God and of one's participation in humanity's refusal—must be shed so that one's self-giving to God can be total and free. The striving for a total self-giving is, of course, both spiritual and moral. Christians strive, with God's help, to unite their lives completely to the life of Christ through the working of the Spirit who prays within them and so brings them to become one with God in prayer. No less, and at the same time, Christians strive to make every decision and action conformable to their surrender to God who is the source of all good.

The totality that Christian conversion seeks requires a lifetime. The experience of conversion is not a once-for-all and final accomplishment; rather, it sets the Christian on a path of ongoing, continual, lifelong conversion. Traditionally this dynamism of ongoing conversion in the Christian life has been understood in terms of the Three Ways of purgation, illumination, and union. In more contemporary terms, it might be described as the dynamism of the ever-increasing realization of the fundamental orientation of one's life toward God. Although their conversion and commitment is deep and sincere, Christians discover that they cannot dispose themselves definitively or completely to God all at once. Thus, there is the unavoidable element of moral and spiritual striving, of asceticism, in every authentic Christian life.

Christian conversion is, of course, centered on the person of Jesus. It is a transformation of the person in Christ that can be described as "being born again," "new life in Christ," or "being in Christ." As Jesus is the perfect revelation of God's love, he is also the perfect revelation of the authentic pattern of the human response to God. The perfect image of God becomes the way for all those created in God's image. The Christian life, then, is a following of Jesus. It is the path of discipleship. This discipleship is more than an external imitation of Jesus; it is, rather, a conforming of oneself to Jesus. It is a becoming one with Christ rooted in prayer and lived out in action:

I have been crucified with Christ, and it is no longer I who
live, but it is Christ who lives in me. And the life I now live in
the flesh I live by faith in the Son of God, who loved me and
gave himself for me (Gal 2:19–20 NRSV).

As a following of Jesus, the disciple's path of ongoing
conversion is necessarily a way of the cross. The disciple's effort
to love as Jesus did, to transcend self in loving self-giving,
unavoidably encounters the difficulties that give such surrender
the character of self-sacrifice. The disciple must learn to go on
trusting in God in order to continue on the path of self-giving
even in the face of the physical evils of sickness, suffering, and
death. And more, the authentic self-giving of the Christian life is
made difficult by the "drag" of the inherited effects of humanity's
refusals to respond to God, by the inauthentic responses
encountered in society, and by the accumulated resistance of
one's own personal sin. To follow Jesus along the path of ongoing
conversion is therefore to embrace the cross of struggling to
overcome sin (in oneself and in the world) and to accept the evil
that cannot be changed.

It is participation in the Christian community that teaches
one the way of Christian discipleship and that enables one to
embrace the lived meaning of conformity to Christ. The community forms men and women for Christian discipleship
through the explicit means of preaching, catechesis, and official
teaching by those charged by God with a teaching ministry; but
there is also the implicit but powerful formation that comes with
prayer within the context of the church, meditation on the word
of God handed on in the community, the living witness of faithful
Christians, and especially participation in the communal
celebration of the liturgy. In the liturgy, the Christian is formed in
the Christian story and so takes on the distinctive self-identity,
character, and virtues of the Christian that will impact all
subsequent decisions and actions.

Also, beyond learning about and being formed in the
Christian way, it is in the church that one finds support to
empower one's discipleship. This empowerment occurs through
explicit witness, encouragement, and challenge; but, once again,

it is in the communal celebration of the liturgy that the Christian is most truly empowered to live as a disciple of Jesus. In the liturgy, the Christian encounters Christ in the midst of the community. And, especially in the eucharist, Christians discover that gratitude is not only the beginning of conversion; it is the ongoing empowerment of a life of conversion.

The vital role that the Christian community plays in Christian discipleship points to the fact that the Christian life is necessarily relational. Obviously, participation in the community implies relation; but more, the life of *theosis*—as the present meaning and future goal of Christian existence—is essentially a life in relationship. The Christian life is directed to participation with other women and men in the triune relationship within the very heart of God. Both as a future hope but also as a present reality, the promise of *theosis* challenges Christians to seek mutuality in relationships. Self-giving in love, especially when realized in true mutuality, mirrors and mediates and anticipates the inner life of God which is the Christian's source and goal. Love of God and love of neighbor are inseparable, in this life and in the next.

The Christian life, therefore, requires the pursuit of authentic relationships—relationships that aim at a full mutuality in self-giving. However, after the model of divine self-giving in Jesus, Christian love does not demand the promise of mutuality as a *precondition* of love. In a world of human limit and sin, Christians accept that full mutuality cannot always be—and perhaps not even often be—fully realized; but Christians are committed to the establishment of the conditions which would make full mutuality possible. They are committed to the establishment of the conditions—interpersonal, social and structural—in which *God* can bring love to full flower in mutuality. Christians, then, are committed to the pursuit of justice, of right relationships, as the precondition of the full mutuality that God will finally accomplish in the final manifestation of God's reign. Any authentic Christian spirituality is necessarily and essentially committed to justice.

The liturgy celebrates the reality and promise of God's invitation to share in the mutual self-giving of the trinitarian love. In the liturgy, Christians celebrate the new relationships that they have with God and with one another in Christ. The celebration of the liturgy, then, necessarily challenges Christians to seek authentic relationships, to seek justice, outside the liturgy and outside the bounds of the Christian community. It forms them as men and women who are familiar with the shape of authentic relationships, and it therefore directs and empowers them to seek the realization of such relationships in the world. At the same time, the Christian pursuit of justice itself also forms the Christian to recognize and to challenge any inauthentic elements in the community's life and in its celebration of liturgy. An authentic Christian spirituality rooted in the liturgy necessarily flows out into moral living.

Of course, the pursuit of authentic relationships must be realized in actions, in decisions. The life of ongoing conversion itself must be realized in decisions and in the actions that flow from them. In fact, since the Christian's most fundamental life direction aims at a *total* response to God, ongoing conversion seeks the ever-increasing realization of this fundamental orientation in every action. At the same time, it seeks the increasing integration of all one's choices into one's most fundamental life commitment. Individual decisions and human actions, therefore, are an important aspect of the Christian's response to God, concrete realizations of this response. In them, the Christian seeks to respond to God's call and invitation.

There must be, then, in the decisions of Christians a spirit of discernment. In each decision, Christians are seeking God's will—that is, an authentic response to God who is always calling them into relationship. Thus, discernment is not some "spiritual technique" added to an otherwise rational process of decision-making; rather, the use of moral rules and reasoning are important but partial ways in which the shape of God's will is revealed in concrete circumstances.

Because the moral decision-making of Christians always involves a discernment of God's will, prayer for guidance and especially a life of prayer are vitally important to decision-making. It is a life of prayer, personal and communal, that forms Christians to make decisions consistent with their identity as disciples of Jesus and as participants in the divine nature.

Through a life of prayer, the Christian becomes attentive, familiar, and docile to the Spirit's promptings—just as loving converse with a human friend brings an intuitive knowledge of the other's desires. The "spiritual" expression of prayer is thus essential to the most concrete expression of the Christian moral life; and it is in decision-making that the relationship of the moral and spiritual life, of ethics and spirituality, has its most concrete expression.

Christian ethics and Christian spirituality are inseparable because the Christian life, Christian discipleship, is a totality. The Christian way is the person's entire life—and nothing less—because the self-giving of God in Christ requires the total response of the Christian in self-giving love. What other human response but the total giving of one's life would be possible to the God who has given "his own only Son" in order to invite and enable sinners to share in the divine life itself?

Christian ethics focuses its attention on Christian character, virtues, decisions, and acts that conform the Christian to the response that Jesus has made to God. Christian spirituality focuses its attention on Christian prayer and all that serves one's communion with God and with others in God. Each discipline has its proper focus. But, as we have seen, there is no separating the Christian's moral striving from his or her spiritual striving. There is no separating one's grateful response to God in moral living from one's response to God in worship and in prayer. Both are aspects of the Christian life aimed at the total surrender of self to God. In sum, then, Christian ethics and Christian spirituality are inseparable because becoming good and becoming holy are intimately and inseparably linked in the Christian response to God.

NOTES

Introduction

1. Vatican II, *Optatam totius* (Decree on the Training of Priests), no. 16, in *Vatican Council II: The Conciliar and Post Conciliar Documents*, ed. Austin Flannery (Collegeville: Liturgical, 1975), 720.

2. Josef Fuchs, "Moral Theology According to Vatican II," in *Human Values and Christian Morality* (Dublin: Gill and Macmillan, 1970), 1–55. Fuchs returns to similar themes in a number of his works. See, for example: "The Christian Morality of Vatican II," in *Human Values*, 56–75; "Moral Theology and Christian Existence" and "Vocation and Hope: Conciliar Orientations for a Christian Morality," in *Personal Responsibility and Christian Morality* (Washington: Georgetown University, 1983), 19–31 and 32–49, respectively.

3. Pope John Paul II, *Veritatis splendor* (Washington: USCC, 1993). See especially chapter one, nos. 6–27, on pages 12–45.

4. Throughout the present work, I will use the terms "moral theology" and "Christian ethics" as interchangeable. Actually, one's choice between the terms can imply a slightly different perspective on the academic discipline that studies the moral life of Christians—although different authors often suggest a different

understanding of these implications. In chapter 1, I will discuss the terms "spirituality" and "spiritual theology," but in the present work I will use the term "spirituality" almost exclusively. In fact, my particular concerns in this book may suggest that the terms "moral theology" and "spiritual theology" are closer to my purposes since I am focusing particularly on the the moral and spiritual lives *of Christians* and on the Christian theological disciplines that study these moral and spiritual lives.

5.   Vatican II, *Lumen gentium*, nos. 39–42, in Flannery, 396–402.

1. Ethics and Spirituality: Past, Present, Future

1.   Donal Dorr, *Spirituality and Justice* (Maryknoll, NY: Orbis, 1984), 8–18.

2.   A helpful perspective on the moral implications of the Bible is provided in Thomas W. Ogeltree, *The Use of the Bible in Christian Ethics* (Philadelphia: Fortress, 1983). For a more detailed study of New Testament literature, see Rudolf Schnackenberg, *The Moral Teaching of the New Testament*, trans. J. Holland-Smith and W.J. O'Hara (New York: Seabury, 1973).

3.   A helpful summary of patristic spirituality is provided by Boniface Ramsey, "The Spirituality of the Early Church: Patristic Sources," in *Spiritual Traditions for the Contemporary Church*, ed. Robin Maas and Gabriel O'Donnell (Nashville: Abingdon, 1990), 25–44. See also Boniface Ramsey, *Beginning to Read the Fathers* (New York: Paulist, 1985), 56–94.

4.   Charles E. Curran, "The Historical Development of Moral Theology," in *Toward an American Catholic Moral Theology* (Notre Dame, IN: University of Notre Dame Press, 1987), 3–6. For more extended histories of Catholic moral theology, see John Mahoney, *The Making of Moral Theology: A Study of the Roman Catholic Tradition* (Oxford: Clarendon Press, 1987); and John A. Gallagher, *Time Past, Time Future: An Historical Study of Catholic Moral Theology* (New York: Paulist, 1990).

5. Yves M.J. Congar, *A History of Theology*, trans. Hunter Guthrie (Garden City, NJ: Doubleday, 1968), 166–70.

6. Some pre-Vatican II manuals of spiritual theology maintained a relative discontinuity between ascetical and mystical states, for example: Adolphe Tanquerey, *The Spiritual Life: A Treatise on Ascetical and Mystical Theology*, trans. Herman Branderis, 2nd. rev. ed. (Westminster: Newman, 1948). Other manuals maintained a greater continuity and thus, it seems, a greater sense of a universal Christian vocation to higher forms of prayer, for example: Reginald Garrigou-Lagrange, *The Three Ages of the Interior Life*, 2 vols., trans. T. Doyle (New York: Herder, 1948).

7. Jon Alexander makes the interesting observation that the first issue of the *Elenchus bibliographicus* of the *Ephemerides theologicae lovanienses* in 1924 placed the category "Theologica Ascetica et Mystica" as a subdivision of "Theologia Moralis." It was in 1951 that "Theologica Ascetica et Mystica" became a separate section. Jon Alexander, "What Do Recent Writers Mean by *Spirituality?*" *Spirituality Today* 32 (September 1980): 250–51.

8. Pierre Pourrat, *Christian Spirituality*, trans. W.H. Mitchell and S.P. Jacques (Westminster: Newman, 1953–55), I:v.

9. Sandra Schneiders, "Theology and Spirituality: Strangers, Rivals, or Partners?" *Horizons* 13 (Fall 1986): 263.

10. One of the earliest contemporary efforts was by the Protestant ethicist, James Gustafson: "Spiritual Life and Moral Life," *Theology Digest* 17 (Winter 1971): 296–307. See also Sergio Bastianel, *Prayer in the Christian Moral Life*, trans. Bernard Hoose (St. Paul Publications, 1988); Michael K. Duffey, *Be Blessed in What You Do: The Unity of Christian Ethics and Spirituality* (New York: Paulist, 1988); William E. May, *The Unity of the Moral and Spiritual Life*, Synthesis series (Chicago: Franciscan Herald Press, 1979); and Enda McDonagh, "Morality and Prayer" and "Morality and Spirituality," in *Doing the Truth: The Quest for Moral Theology* (Notre Dame: University of Notre Dame Press, 1979), 40–75.

11. Vatican II, *Optatam totius*, no. 16, in *Vatican II: The Conciliar and Post Conciliar Documents*, ed. Austin Flannery (Collegeville: Liturgical, 1975), 720.

12. See Romanus Cessario, *The Moral Virtues and Theological Ethics* (Notre Dame: University of Notre Dame Press, 1991).

13. McDonagh, 58.

14. While the discussion of the two forms of human response to God can be found in Häring's recent work, it can be found most prominently in his doctoral dissertation, later published as his first book, *Das Heilige und das Gute*, in 1954.

15. See, for example, Richard M. Gula, *Reason Informed by Faith: Foundations of Catholic Morality* (New York: Paulist, 1989), 7–8; and Timothy E. O'Connell, *Principles for a Catholic Morality*, rev. ed. (San Francisco: Harper and Row, 1990), 254–55.

16. McDonagh, 59.

17. James Gustafson, "The Focus and Its Limitations: Reflections on Catholic Moral Theology," in *Moral Theology: Challenges for the Future*, ed. Charles E. Curran (New York: Paulist, 1990), 181. Gustafson goes on to reflect on the limitations of this narrow focus (pp. 181–89).

18. John Heagle, "A New Public Piety: Reflections on Spirituality," *Church* 1 (Fall 1985): 52–53.

19. See, for example, two important articles by Sandra Schneiders: "Theology and Spirituality: Strangers, Rivals or Partners?" *Horizons* 13 (Fall 1986): 253–74; and "Spirituality in the Academy," in *Modern Christian Spirituality*, ed. Bradley C. Hanson, American Academy of Religion Studies in Religion 62 (Atlanta: Scholars Press, 1990), 15–37. Articles by Ewert H. Cousins, Bradley C. Hanson, and Carlos M.N. Eire in the latter volume also provide helpful examinations of the present state of the discipline of

Christian spirituality. See also Walter Principe, "Toward Defining Spirituality," *Studies in Religion/Sciences Religieuses* 12 (1983): 127–41.

20. Michael Downey, "Understanding Christian Spirituality: Dress Rehearsal for a Method," *Spirituality Today* (Autumn 1991): 273–77.

21. See, for example, Jay B. McDaniel, *Earth, Sky, Gods, and Mortals: Developing an Ecological Spirituality* (Mystic, CT: Twenty-Third Publications, 1990).

22. See, for example, two books by Donal Dorr: *Spirituality and Justice* (Maryknoll: Orbis, 1984) and *Integral Spirituality: Resources for Community, Peace, Justice and the Earth* (Maryknoll: Orbis, 1990).

23. There are already a significant number of works on liberation spirituality. See, for example, Gustavo Gutiérrez, *We Drink from Our Own Wells: The Spiritual Journey of a People* (Maryknoll: Orbis, 1984); Jon Sobrino, *Spirituality of Liberation: Toward a Political Holiness* (Maryknoll: Orbis, 1985); Segundo Galilea, *The Way of Living Faith: A Spirituality of Liberation* (San Francisco: Harper and Row, 1988); and Nestor Jaen, *Toward a Liberation Spirituality* (Chicago: Loyola University Press, 1991).

24. Schneiders, "Theology and Spirituality," 266.

2. Conversion at the Heart of Christian Life

1. The absence of any explicit discussion of biblical views of conversion will confirm that this chapter does not pretend to offer a complete theology of conversion. For biblical views, see Michael H. Crosby, "The Biblical Vision of Conversion," in *The Human Experience of Conversion: Persons and Structures in Transformation*, ed. Francis A. Eigo (Villanova, PA: Villanova University Press, 1987), 31–74; Michael Brennen Dick, "Conversion in the Bible," in *Conversion and the Catechumenate*, ed. Robert Duggan (New York: Paulist, 1984), 43–63; Beverly Roberts Gaventa, *From Darkness to*

Light: Aspects of Conversion in the New Testament (Philadelphia: Fortress, 1986); Ronald D. Witherup, *Conversion in the New Testament* (Collegeville, MN: Michael Glazier, 1994).

2. Bernard Lonergan, *Method in Theology* (New York: Seabury, 1972).

3. See, for example, Walter Conn, *Christian Conversion: A Developmental Interpretation of Autonomy and Surrender* (New York: Paulist, 1986); Donald L. Gelpi, *Charism and Sacrament: A Theology of Christian Conversion* (New York: Paulist, 1976); and *Committed Worship: A Sacramental Theology for Converting Christians*, vol. 1: *Adult Conversion and Initiation* (Collegeville, MN: Michael Glazier, 1993); and Stephen Happel and James J. Walter, *Conversion and Discipleship: A Christian Foundation for Ethics and Doctrine* (Philadelphia: Fortress, 1986).

4. Lonergan, 130–31.

5. Lonergan, 131.

6. Lonergan, 238–40.

7. Lonergan, 240.

8. Conn, *Christian Conversion*, 113.

9. Happel and Walter, 39.

10. Conn, *Christian Conversion*, 134–35.

11. Conn, *Christian Conversion*, 134–35, 147–50. See also Walter Conn, "The Desire for Authenticity: Conscience and Moral Conversion," in *The Desires of the Human Heart: An Introduction to the Theology of Bernard Lonergan*, ed. Vernon Gregson (New York: Paulist, 1988), 52–53.

12. Conn says: "Affective conversion, therefore, is the concrete possibility of overcoming moral impotence, of not only being able

to make a decision to commit oneself to a course of action or direction of life judged worthwhile and personally appropriate, but of being able to execute that decision over the long haul against serious obstacles." Conn, "Desire for Authenticity," 53.

13. Lonergan, 240.

14. According to Lonergan (*Method*, 241), "...what sublates goes beyond what is sublated, introduces something new and distinct, puts everything on a new basis, yet so far from interfering with the sublated or destroying it, on the contrary needs it, includes it, preserves all its proper features and properties, and carries them forward to a fuller realization within a richer context."

15. Lonergan, 243. Elsewhere (pp. 267–68) Lonergan says: "Foundational reality, as distinct from its expression, is conversion: religious, moral, and intellectual. Normally, it is intellectual conversion as the fruit of both religious and moral conversion; it is moral conversion as the fruit of religious conversion; and it is religious conversion as the fruit of God's gift of his grace."

16. Lonergan, 106.

17. See Brian V. Johnstone, "The Experience of Conversion and the Foundations of Moral Theology," *Église et Théologie* 15 (1984): 199–200.

18. Johnstone, 200.

19. Denise Lardner Carmody says: "In my view, the key to a Lonerganian notion of Christian conversion is specifying religious love, being in love in an unrestricted fashion, through the person and program of Jesus Christ." Carmody, "The Desire for Transcendence: Religious Conversion," in *The Desires of the Human Heart*, 71.

20. Conn, *Christian Conversion*, 193–95, 216–28.

21. Conn, *Christian Conversion*, 159.

22. Conn, *Christian Conversion*, 198.

23. Conn, *Christian Conversion*, 334, fn. 40.

24. Lonergan, 284; Carmody, 63.

25. See William Thompson, *Fire and Light: The Saints and Theology* (New York: Paulist, 1987).

26. Bernard Häring, *Free and Faithful in Christ: Moral Theology for Clergy and Laity* (New York: Seabury, 1978), I:62–67.

27. Frank Fletcher, "Mutual Self-Mediation in Christ," in *Australian Lonergan Workshop*, ed. William J. Danaher (Lanham, MD: University Press of America, 1993), 81.

28. Regis A. Duffy, "The Praxis of Conversion," in *Initiation and Conversion*, ed. Lawrence J. Johnson (Collegeville, MN: Liturgical Press, 1985), 17–20.

29. Bernard Häring, *This Time of Salvation* (New York: Herder and Herder, 1966), 219–23; Charles E. Curran, "Conversion: The Central Moral Message of Jesus," in *A New Look at Christian Morality* (Notre Dame, IN: Fides, 1970), 25–71.

30. Joann Wolski Conn and Walter E. Conn, "Discerning Conversion," *The Way Supplement* 64 (Spring 1989): 64.

31. Jim Wallis, *The Call to Conversion* (San Francisco: Harper and Row, 1982), 1.

32. Gelpi, *Committed Worship*, 46–51; and Donald Gelpi, "Religious Conversion: A New Way of Being," in *The Human Experience of Conversion*, 180–83. See also Conn, *Christian Conversion*, 203–5.

33. Edward K. Braxton speaks of an "ecclesial conversion." See Braxton, "Dynamics of Conversion," in *Conversion and the*

Catechumenate, 113–14. See also Häring's discussion of the church as "the sacrament of conversion" in *Free and Faithful*, 1:426–29.

34. Gelpi, *Committed Worship*, 76.

35. Lonergan, 241.

36. Richard Byrne, "Journey: Growth and Development in Spiritual Life," in *The New Dictionary of Catholic Spirituality*, ed. Michael Downey (Collegeville, MN: Michael Glazier, 1993), 565–77.

37. Häring, 1:215–18. Although a later chapter focuses on funda-mental option, it might be noted here that Pope John Paul accepts certain aspects of fundamental option theory but strongly rejects others. See his recent encyclical letter *Veritatis splendor*: Regarding Fundamental Questions of the Church's Moral Teaching, nos. 65–70 (Washington: USCC, 1993), 98–108.

38. Josef Fuchs, "Sin and Conversion," in *Introduction to Christian Ethics: A Reader*, ed. Ronald P. Hamel and Kenneth R. Himes (New York: Paulist, 1989), 215. The article originally appeared in English in *Theology Digest* 14 (Winter 1966): 292–301.

39. Conn, *Christian Conversion*, 199–200.

40. Fuchs, 213.

3. Dynamism and Integration:
Fundamental Option and the Three Ways

1. In addition to the sources to be cited below, see Eugene Cooper, "A Newer Look at the Theology of Sin," *Louvain Studies* 3 (Fall 1971): 259–307; Eugene Cooper, "The Notion of Sin in Light of the Theory of the Fundamental Option: The Fundamental Option Revisited," *Louvain Studies* 9 (Fall 1983): 363–82; and John W. Glaser, "Transition Between Grace and Sin: Fresh Perspectives," *Theological Studies* 29 (June 1968): 260–74.

2. Bernard Häring, *Free and Faithful in Christ* (New York: Seabury, 1978), I:164–222.

3. Joseph Fuchs, *Human Values and Christian Morality* (Dublin: Gill and Macmillan, 1970), 92–111.

4. Karl Rahner, *Theological Investigations* (New York: Crossroad, 1982), VI:178–96; *Foundations of Christian Faith* (New York: Crossroad, 1982), 90–115.

5. See, for example, articles in: William E. May, ed., *Principles of Catholic Moral Life* (Chicago: Franciscan Herald Press, 1980), 193–266. For a response to these critics, see Richard A. McCormick, *The Critical Calling* (Washington: Georgetown University Press, 1989), 171–90. Pope John Paul II has also raised concerns about fundamental option theory in two official pronouncements: his 1984 apostolic exhortation, *Reconciliation and penance*, no. 17 (Washington: USCC, 1984), 56–64; and in his 1993 encyclical, *Veritatis splendor*, nos. 65–70 (Washington: USCC, 1993), 98–108. While acknowledging the validity of the basic language of fundamental option, he warns against certain tendencies that he perceives in forms of fundamental option thinking. Specifically, the pope warns against any suggestion that there can be an actual *separation* between a fundamental life commitment and individual exercises of free choice. This tendency would suggest that one could commit gravely disordered acts without true moral consequence for the agent. Against any such tendency, Pope John Paul reaffirms the traditional teaching that people can sin in an individual act, that sinful acts are either mortal or venial, and that mortal sin is not to be understood as a rare occurrence in the life of Christians. For a response by a proponent of fundamental option theory, see Josef Fuchs, "Good Acts and Good Persons," *The Tablet* 247 (November 6, 1993): 1444–45.

6. See Aldolphe Tanquerey, *The Spiritual Life: A Treatise on Ascetical and Mystical Theology* (Westminster, MD: Newman, 1948), 297–750; Joseph de Guibert, *The Theology of the Spiritual Life* (New York: Sheed and Ward, 1953), 265–301; Louis Bouyer, *Introduction*

to Spirituality (New York: Desclée, 1961), 243–85; Louis Dupré, *The Deeper Life: An Introduction to Christian Mysticism* (New York: Crossroad, 1981).

7. Rahner, *Theological Investigations*, VI:189–90. See also *Theological Investigations*, V:439–59, VI:231–49.

4. Goal and Present Reality: Participation in Divine Life

1. James R. Pollack, "Horizons in Moral Theology," in *Chicago Studies* 28 (Nov. 1989): 340–41.

2. See, for example, Henry Davis, *Moral and Pastoral Theology*, 4th ed. (London: Sheed and Ward, 1945), vol. 1.

3. See, for example, Vladimir Lossky, *The Mystical Theology of the Eastern Church* (London: James Clarke and Co., 1957); A Monk of the Eastern Church, *Orthodox Spirituality: An Outline of the Orthodox Ascetical and Mystical Tradition* (London: SPCK, 1945); and John Meyendorff, "Theosis in the Eastern Christian Tradition," in *Christian Spirituality*, III: *Post-Reformation and Modern*, ed. Louis Dupré and Don E. Saliers (New York: Crossroad, 1991), 470–76. For a more popular treatment, see Christoforos Stavropoulos, *Partakers of Divine Nature*, trans. Stanley Harakas (Minneapolis: Light and Life, 1976).

4. See, for example, Vigen Guroian, *Incarnate Love: Essays in Orthodox Ethics* (Notre Dame, IN: University of Notre Dame Press, 1987); Stanley S. Harakas, *Toward Transfigured Life: The Theoria of Eastern Orthodox Ethics* (Minneapolis: Light and Life, 1983); and Christos Yannaras, *The Freedom of Morality* (Crestwood, NY: St. Vladimir's Seminary Press, 1984). Guroian's work is the first English language work on Orthodox ethics to be published by a non-Orthodox publisher in the United States. It is more explicitly in dialogue with non-Orthodox ethics and shows the influence of the character ethics of Protestant ethicist Stanley Hauerwas. For an explicit treatment of Eastern *Catholic* thought, see George Appleyard, David Petras, and Fred Saato, *Shown to Be Holy: An*

Introduction to Eastern Christian Moral Thought (McKees Rocks, PA: God with Us, 1990).

5. See, for example, Nicholas Cabasilas, *The Life in Christ*, trans. Carmino J. DeCatanzaro (Crestwood, NY: St. Vladimir's Seminary Press, 1974); Georgios I. Mantzaridis, *The Deification of Man: St. Gregory Palamas and the Orthodox Tradition* (Crestwood, NY: St. Vladimir's Seminary Press, 1984); Thomas Hopko, "The Trinity in the Cappadocians," in *Christian Spirituality*, I: *Origins to the Twelfth Century*, ed. Bernard McGinn, John Meyendorff, and Jean LeClerq (New York: Crossroad, 1989), 260–76; George Mantzaridis, "Spiritual Life in Palamism," in *Christian Spirituality*, II: *High Middle Ages and Reformation*, ed. Jill Raitt (New York: Crossroad, 1989), 208–22; Andrew Louth, "Maximus the Confessor," in *The Study of Spirituality*, ed. Cheslyn Jones, Geoffrey Wainwright, and Edward Yarnold (New York: Oxford University Press, 1984), 190–95.

6. For a historical survey of the development of the concept of *theosis* in both East and West, see "Divinisation" in *Dictionnaire de Spiritualité* (Paris: Beauchesne, 1957), vol. 3, cols. 1370–1459. For a brief contemporary Roman Catholic discussion of deification, see International Theological Commission, "Theology, Christology, Anthropology," in *International Theological Commission: Texts and Documents, 1969–85*, ed. Michael Sharkey (San Francisco: Ignatius, 1989), 215–16. An Anglican perspective is offered by A.M. Allchin, *Participation in God: A Forgotten Strand in Anglican Tradition* (Wilton, CT: Morehouse-Barlow, 1988). A Lutheran perspective is suggested by Michael C.D. McDaniel, "Salvation as Justification and *Theosis*," in *Salvation in Christ: A Lutheran-Orthodox Dialogue*, ed. John Meyendorff and Robert Tobias (Minneapolis: Augsburg, 1992).

7. Catherine Mowry LaCugna, *God for Us: The Trinity and Christian Life* (San Francisco: Harper and Row, 1991), 10.

8. Vladimir Lossky, *In the Image and Likeness of God*, ed. John H. Erickson and Thomas E. Bird (Crestwood, NY: St. Vladimir's

Seminary Press, 1974), 125–39; Lossky, *Mystical*, pp. 114–34; and Dumitru Staniloae, "Image, Likeness, and Deification in the Human Person," *Communio* 13 (Spring 1986): 64–83. Roman Catholic anthropology also begins with an affirmation of the human person as *imago Dei*, but it does not function with precisely the same emphases. For a Western perspective on the human person as image of God, see D. Juvenal Merriell, *To the Image of the Trinity: A Study in the Development of Aquinas' Teaching* (Toronto: Pontifical Institute of Medieval Studies, 1990); and John Edward Sullivan, *The Image of God: The Doctrine of St. Augustine and Its Influence* (Dubuque, IA: The Priory Press, 1963), esp. 288–307. See also Lars Thunberg, "The Human Person as Image of God: Eastern Christianity," in *Christian Spirituality*, I:291–312; Bernard McGinn, "The Human Person as Image of God: Western Christianity," in *Christian Spirituality*, I:312–30.

9. The International Theological Commission (p. 216) in its brief discussion of deification summarizes: "In this sense deification properly understood can make man perfectly human: deification is the truest and ultimate hominization of man."

10. See, for example, Thunberg, 291–312; Lossky, *Mystical*, 114–34; Lossky, *Image*, 125–39; Mantzaridis, "Spiritual Life," 21–23.

11. Harakas, 21–22.

12. Lossky, *Image*, 97–98; Lossky, *Mystical*, 136–37.

13. Lossky, *Image*, 110. See chapter 5, "Redemption and Deification," 97–110.

14. Harakas, 36, 147.

15. See especially Panayiotis Nellas, *Deification in Christ: The Nature of the Human Person* (Crestwood, NY: St. Vladimir's Seminary Press, 1987). See also Monk of the Eastern Church, 57–59.

16. Mantzaridis, "Spiritual Life," 35.

17. Lossky, *Image*, 109; Lossky, *Mystical*, 135–73; Mantzaridis, "Spiritual Life," 25–39.

18. Harakas, 229–71.

19. Lossky, *Mystical*, 207. See also Mantzaridis, "Spiritual Life," 87–93.

20. Lossky, *Mystical*, 202–206.

21. Guroian, 16. Guroian's summary closely parallels Bernard Lonergan's idea that moral conversion is "sublated"—taken up without loss—in religious conversion, that is an "otherworldly falling in love." See Bernard J.F. Lonergan, *Method in Theology* (New York: Seabury, 1972), 241.

22. Harakas, 40–67.

23. Harakas, 199–205.

24. Harakas, 179–211; Guroian, 13–28.

25. Harakas, 37, 146–47.

26. Guroian, 31–34; Staniloae, 80–83.

27. Guroian, 22–26.

28. Mantzaridis, "Spiritual Life," 57–60.

29. Paul Meyendorff, "Liturgy and Spirituality: Eastern Liturgical Theology," in *Christian Spirituality* I:350–63; Guroian, 51–78; Mantzaridis, "Spiritual Life," 41–60. The Second Vatican Council also emphasized the centrality of liturgy and sacrament in the life of the church. See chapter eight.

30. Several historical factors may be suggested as reasons for the

Western discomfort with the concept of deification. The first may be the fear of a possible association with the ideas of certain sectarian and apocalyptic groups of the Middle Ages and of the later radical reformation that claimed the attainment of a union with the essence of God and thus of a sinlessness in the present life. The second may be the possibility of confusion between a concept of deification and certain speculations about "a divine and uncreated 'core' of the human soul." See Rowan Williams, "Deification," in *The Westminster Dictionary of Christian Spirituality*, ed. Gordon S. Wakefield (Philadelphia: Westminster, 1983), 106–108. Further, Western anthropology, following on Augustine's effort to counter the excessive optimism of Pelagianism, placed a relatively greater emphasis on original sin than did Eastern anthropology. In this Western theological context and in the context of the apparent collapse of Roman civilization in the West, "becoming God" may have seemed a far more distant goal for fallen humanity. See also Bernard McGinn, "Christ as Savior in the West," in *Christian Spirituality*, I:253–59.

31. See Gustave Bardy et al., "Divinisation" in the *Dictionnaire de Spiritualité*, vol. III, cols. 1389–1459.

32. See, for example, Adolphe Tanquerey, *The Spiritual Life: A Treatise on Ascetical and Mystical Theology*, 2nd ed. (Westminster, MD: Newman, 1948).

33. See, for example, Ben Drewery, "Deification," in *Christian Spirituality: Essays in Honour of Gordon Rupp*, ed. Peter Brooks (London: SCM, 1975), 35–62.

34. Meyendorff, "Theosis," 470–72.

35. LaCugna, 10.

36. A full discussion of the trinitarian roots of the Eastern Christian understanding of *theosis* and of its possible reappropriation in the West could not ignore the differences in trinitarian theology that have long separated East and West. The fact that the

present study does not elaborate these differences is not meant to suggest that these differences are in any way insignificant. See Lossky, *Image*, 71–96; Lossky, *Mystical*, 44–66; Thomas Hopko, "The Trinity in the Cappadocians," in *Christian Spirituality*, I:260–76; Mary T. Clark, "The Trinity in Latin Christianity," in *Christian Spirituality* I:276–90; Thomas R. Martland, "Cappadocian and Augustinian Trinitarian Methodology," *Anglican Theological Review* 47 (July 1965): 252–63.

37. Lossky, *Mystical*, 67–90. For a critical comment, see LaCugna, 287.

38. William M. Thompson, *Christology and Spirituality* (New York: Crossroad, 1991), 87–100.

39. Catherine Mowry LaCugna, *God for Us: The Trinity and Christian Life* (San Francisco: Harper and Row, 1991).

40. Thompson, 87–100. Thompson notes the summary offered by the Pontifical Biblical Commission in a 1984 statement which includes a discussion of Christologies "from above" and "from below": "All attempts to unite a *Christology 'from below' with a Christology 'from above'* are on the right track." For an English translation and commentary on the statement, see Joseph A. Fitzmyer, *Scripture and Christology: A Statement of the Biblical Commission with a Commentary* (New York: Paulist, 1986), 29.

41. Lossky (*Mystical*, p. 215) expresses some caution about understanding the Christian life as an "imitation of Christ" since the way of Christ himself was one of descent through *kenosis*, while the way of the Christian is one of ascent through *theosis*. On the other hand, see Monk of the Eastern Church, 56–57.

42. LaCugna, 284–88. LaCugna's critique of the implications of Orthodox trinitarian theology and its relationship to eschatology would be important to address for a more complete appropriation of the Orthodox discussions of deification and the triune God. The critique, however, does not prevent LaCugna from

holding *theosis* as a primary way to understand Christian life: "The life of holiness to which all believers in Christ are called is *theosis*: simply, becoming Christ, becoming deified or 'ingodded.' Only the *Holy Spirit* can make us holy; only God can divinize us, conform us more perfectly to the very life of God" (p. 409).

43. Leonardo Boff, *Trinity and Society*, trans. Paul Burns (Maryknoll, NY: Orbis, 1988). Boff offers a "nutshell" summary of the implications for liberation in an authentic trinitarian understanding on pages 236–37.

44. LaCugna, 285–87.

45. For a brief summary of the contemporary discussion of models, see Richard M. Gula, *Reason Informed by Faith: Foundations of Catholic Morality* (New York: Paulist, 1989), 300–306.

46. See, for example, Bernard Häring, *Free and Faithful in Christ* (New York: Seabury, 1978), I:59–103. See also LaCugna's discussion of "Doxology as a Way of Life" on pages 342–48.

5. Authentic Relationships: Justice and Love

1. See, for example, Robert McAfee Brown, *Spirituality and Liberation: Overcoming the Great Fallacy* (Louisville, KY: Westminster, 1988); and Donal Dorr, *Spirituality and Justice* (Maryknoll, NY: Orbis, 1984). The connection between spirituality and justice is also made explicit by Latin American liberation spirituality. See, for example, Segundo Galilea, *The Way of Living Faith: A Spirituality of Liberation* (San Francisco: Harper and Row, 1988); Gustavo Gutierrez, *We Drink from Our Own Wells: The Spiritual Journey of a People* (Maryknoll, NY: Orbis, 1984); Jon Sobrino, *Spirituality of Liberation: Toward Political Holiness* (Maryknoll, NY: Orbis, 1988).

2. John R. Donahue, "Biblical Perspectives on Justice," in *The Faith That Does Justice: Examining the Christian Sources for Social Change*, ed. John C. Haughey (New York: Paulist, 1977), 68–112.

For other discussions of the relational basis of biblical views of justice, see: Stephen Charles Mott, "Egalitarian Aspects of the Biblical Theory of Justice," *American Society of Christian Ethics: Selected Papers (1978)*: 8–26; Mott, *Biblical Ethics and Social Change* (New York: Oxford University Press, 1982), 59–81; Jose Miranda, *Marx and the Bible: A Critique of the Philosophy of Oppression* (Maryknoll, NY: Orbis, 1974); Leslie Hoppe, "Community and Justice: A Biblical Perspective," in *Economic Justice: CTU's Pastoral Commentary on the Bishops' Letter on the Economy*, ed. John Pawlikowski and Donald Senior (Washington, DC: Pastoral Press, 1988), 11–17).

3. Mott, "Egalitarian Aspects," 12.

4. Mott, *Biblical Ethics*, 63.

5. James Luther Mays, "Justice: Perspectives from the Prophetic Tradition," *Interpretation* 37 (January 1983): 5–17.

6. Michael H. Crosby, *House of Disciples: Church, Economics, and Justice in Matthew* (Maryknoll, NY: Orbis, 1988), 216–28.

7. John F. Haught, *The Promise of Nature: Ecology and Cosmic Promise* (New York: Paulist, 1993).

8. Mays, 10–11.

9. Daniel C. Maguire, "The Primacy of Justice in Moral Theology," *Horizons* 10 (Spring 1983): 72–85.

10. David Hollenbach, "Modern Catholic Teachings Concerning Justice," in *Justice, Peace, and Human Rights: American Catholic Social Ethics in a Pluralistic Context* (New York: Crossroad, 1988), 16–33.

11. Karen Lebacqz, *Justice in an Unjust World: Foundations for a Christian Approach to Justice* (Minneapolis: Augsburg, 1987), 176, fn. 61.

12. Gene Outka, *Agape: An Ethical Analysis* (New Haven, CT: Yale University Press, 1972).

13. Jean Porter, "*De Ordine Caritatis:* Charity, Friendship, and Justice in Thomas Aquinas' *Summa Theologiae*," *Thomist* 53 (April 1989): 197–213.

14. Enda McDonagh, "Love, Power, and Justice," in *The Making of Disciples: Tasks of Moral Theology* (Wilmington: Michael Glazier, 1982), 112–27.

15. Outka (24–34) analyzes the difficulties that arise for an understanding of justice when love is understood as self-sacrifice. See also Karen Lebacqz, *Six Theories of Justice: Perspectives from Philosophical and Theological Ethics* (Minneapolis, MN: Augsburg, 1986), 83–99.

16. Hollenbach (18–22) argues that the modern Catholic tradition on justice has emphasized the relational nature of justice and its connection with mutuality, reciprocity, and love.

17. John P. Langan, "What Jerusalem Says to Athens," in *The Faith That Does Justice: Examining the Christian Sources for Social Change*, ed. John C. Haughey (New York: Paulist, 1977), 152–80.

18. Stephen J. Pope, "Aquinas on Almsgiving, Justice, and Charity: An Interpretation and Reassessment," *Heythrop Journal* (1991): 170.

19. My understanding of spirituality is dependent on definitions of spirituality and of *Christian* spirituality offered by Sandra Schneiders in "Theology and Spirituality: Strangers, Rivals, or Partners?" *Horizons* 13 (Fall 1986): 266.

20. Francis X. Meehan, *A Contemporary Social Spirituality* (Maryknoll, NY: Orbis, 1982).

21. Terry Tastard, *The Spark in the Soul: Four Mystics on Justice* (Mahwah, NJ: Paulist, 1989), 113.

22. Tastard, 95–115.

23. For discussion of the implication of this text for Christian spirituality, see Donal Dorr, *Spirituality and Justice*, 8–18; Brown, 67–72.

24. Walter Brueggemann, "Voices of the Night—Against Justice," in *To Act Justly, Love Tenderly, Walk Humbly: An Agenda for Ministers* by Walter Brueggemann, Sharon Parks, and Thomas H. Groome (Mahwah, NJ: Paulist, 1986), 2.

25. Brueggemann, 14–17.

6. Liturgy and Christian Living

1. Vatican II, *Sacrosanctum concilium* (Constitution on the Sacred Liturgy), nos. 9–10, in Austin Flannery, ed., *Vatican II: The Conciliar and Post Conciliar Documents* (Collegeville: Liturgical, 1975), 6.

2. Shawn Madigan, *Spirituality Rooted in the Liturgy* (Washington: Pastoral, 1988); Don E. Saliers, *Worship and Spirituality*, Spirituality and Christian Life series (Philadelphia: Westminster, 1984). See also the collections of articles in: Eleanor Bernstein, ed., *Liturgy and Spirituality in Context: Perspectives on Prayer and Culture* (Collegeville: Liturgical, 1990); and Lawrence J. Johnson, ed., *Called to Prayer: Liturgical Spirituality Today* (Collegeville: Liturgical, 1986).

3. See, for example, both Häring's first and his more recent comprehensive discussions of Catholic moral theology: *The Law of Christ: Moral Theology for Priests and Laity* (Westminster: Newman, 1961), I:35–59; and *Free and Faithful in Christ: Moral Theology for Clergy and Laity* (New York: Seabury, 1978), I:59–103.

4. Among Häring's spiritual and sacramental works are: *A Sacramental Spirituality* (New York: Sheed and Ward, 1965); *The Sacraments and Your Everyday Life* (Liguori, MO: Liguori, 1976);

The Eucharist and Our Everyday Life (New York: Seabury, 1979); and *Prayer: Integration of Faith and Life* (Notre Dame: Fides, 1974).

5.   For a discussion of the connection between sacramental worship and conversion, see Donald L. Gelpi, *Committed Worship: A Sacramental Theology for Converting Christians*, 2 vols. (Collegeville: Glazier/Liturgical, 1993). See also Michael Downey, *Clothed in Christ: The Sacraments and Christian Living* (New York: Crossroad, 1987).

6.   Paul Ramsey, "Liturgy and Ethics," *Journal of Religious Ethics* 7 (Fall 1979): 139–71. The entire issue of the journal was devoted to the relationship of liturgy and ethics. Many of the articles are foundational for later reflections by liturgists and ethicists, and they will be cited in the pages ahead.

7.   See, for example: Gustavo Gutiérrez, *A Theology of Liberation*, rev. ed. (Maryknoll: Orbis, 1990), 5–12; and Gutiérrez, *We Drink from Our Own Wells: The Spiritual Journey of a People* (Maryknoll: Orbis, 1984), 45–51.

8.   Enda McDonagh, "Liturgy," in *The Making of Disciples: Tasks of Moral Theology* (Wilmington, DE: Michael Glazier, 1982), 39.

9.   H. Kathleen Hughes, "Liturgy and Justice: An Intrinsic Relationship," in *Living No Longer for Ourselves: Liturgy and Justice in the Nineties*, eds. Kathleen Hughes and Mark R. Francis (Collegeville: Liturgical, 1991), 49–51.

10. Timothy F. Sedgwick, *Sacramental Ethics: Paschal Identity and the Christian Life* (Philadelphia: Fortress, 1987), 24. As Sedgwick's subtitle suggests, the paschal identity of Christians rooted in the sacramental liturgy is a major theme of his book.

11. Michael Downey, *Clothed in Christ: The Sacraments and Christian Living* (New York: Crossroad, 1987), 36.

12. Sedgwick, 15.

13. Mary Margaret Kelleher, "Liturgy and Christian Imagination," *Worship* 66 (March 1992): 129.

14. Philip J. Rossi, "Narrative, Worship, and Ethics: Empowering Images for the Shape of the Christian Moral Life," *Journal of Religious Ethics* 7 (Fall 1979): 242.

15. Rossi, 243.

16. Kelleher, 128–29. See also: David Hollenbach, "A Prophetic Church and the Sacramental Imagination," in *Justice, Peace, and Human Rights: American Catholic Social Ethics in a Pluralistic Context* (New York: Crossroad, 1988), 181–202; and especially Philip S. Keane, *Christian Ethics and Imagination: A Theological Inquiry* (New York: Paulist, 1984).

17. Paul J. Wadell, "What Do All Those Masses Do for Us? Reflections on the Christian Moral Life and the Eucharist," in *Living No Longer for Ourselves* (Collegeville: Liturgical, 1991), 153–69.

18. Bernard Lonergan, *Method in Theology* (New York: Seabury, 1972), 243.

19. See chapter four ("The Spirit of Response-to-Value in the Liturgy") in Dietrich von Hildebrand, *Liturgy and Personality*, rev. ed. (Baltimore: Helicon, 1960), 46–65.

20. McDonagh, "Liturgy," 41–45.

21. McDonagh develops this point more extensively in "The Meaning and Structure of Moral Experience," in *Gift and Call: Towards a Christian Theology of Morality* (St. Meinrad, IN: Abbey Press, 1975), 17–39.

22. Don E. Saliers, "Liturgy and Ethics: Some New Beginnings," *Journal of Religious Ethics* 7 (Fall 1979): 173–89.

23. Richard A. McCormick, *Notes on Moral Theology 1981–1984* (Lanham, MD: University Press of America, 1984), 17–27.

24. Hughes, 37.

25. McDonagh, "Liturgy," 49.

26. William W. Everett, "Liturgy and Ethics: A Response to Saliers and Ramsey," *Journal of Religious Ethics* 7 (Fall 1979): 208.

27. Margaret A. Farley, "Beyond the Formal Principle: A Reply to Ramsey and Saliers," *Journal of Religious Ethics* 7 (Fall 1979): 191–202.

28. See, for example, James L. Empereur and Christopher G. Kiesling, *The Liturgy That Does Justice*, Theology and Life Series, 33 (Collegeville: Glazier/Liturgical, 1990); Mark Searle, ed., *Liturgy and Social Justice* (Collegeville: Liturgical, 1980); and Edward M. Grosz, ed., *Liturgy and Social Justice: Celebrating Rites—Proclaiming Rights* (Collegeville: Liturgical, 1989).

29. Tissa Balasuriya, *The Eucharist and Human Liberation* (Maryknoll: Orbis, 1979); and Monika K. Hellwig, *The Eucharist and the Hunger of the World*, 2nd ed. (Kansas City: Sheed and Ward, 1992).

30. Dianne Bergant, "Liturgy and Scripture: Creating a New World," in *Liturgy and Social Justice: Celebrating Rites—Proclaiming Rights*, 12–25; Eugene LaVerdiere, "Worship and Ethical Responsibility," in *To Do Justice and Right upon the Earth*, Papers from the Virgil Michel Symposium on Liturgy and Social Justice, ed. Mary E. Stamps (Collegeville: Liturgical, 1993), 16–32.

31. See also Isaiah 1:11–17; Hosea 6:6; Micah 6:6–8.

32. LaVerdiere, 20.

33. R. Kevin Seasoltz, "Liturgy and Social Consciousness," in *To Do Justice and Right*, 53.

34. Hans Bernhard Meyer, "The Social Significance of the Liturgy," in *Politics and Liturgy*, Concilium 92, eds. Herman Schmidt and David Power (New York: Herder and Herder, 1974), 41.

35. John J. Egan, *Liturgy and Justice: An Unfinished Agenda* (Collegeville: Liturgical, 1983); Theodore Ross, "The Personal Synthesis of Liturgy and Justice: Five Portraits," in *Living No Longer for Ourselves*, 21–24; R.W. Franklin and Robert L. Spaeth, *Virgil Michel: American Catholic* (Collegeville: Liturgical, 1988), 90–103; Paul B. Marx, *Virgil Michel and the Liturgical Movement* (Collegeville: Liturgical, 1957), 176–218; Kenneth R. Himes, "Eucharist and Justice: Assessing the Legacy of Virgil Michel," *Worship* 62 (May 1988): 201–24.

36. Egan, 3.

37. Egan, 22–23.

38. J. Bryan Hehir, "Liturgy and Social Justice: Past Relationships and Future Possibilities," in *Liturgy and Social Justice: Celebrating Rites—Proclaiming Rights*, 40–61.

39. National Conference of Catholic Bishops, *Economic Justice for All: A Pastoral Letter on Catholic Social Teaching and the U.S. Economy* (1986), nos. 329–31, in *Catholic Social Thought: The Documentary Heritage*, eds. David J. O'Brien and Thomas A. Shannon (Maryknoll: Orbis, 1992), 655.

40. Hughes, 39–44; Mark Searle, "Serving the Lord with Justice," in *Liturgy and Social Justice*, 13–35.

41. McDonagh, "Liturgy," 57–59.

42. Hollenbach, 195.

43. Bergant, 14.

44. William R. Crockett, *Eucharist: Symbol of Transformation* (New York: Pueblo, 1989), 256.

45. Raymond Hunthausen, "Homily for the Opening Session," in *Liturgy and Social Justice: Celebrating Rites—Proclaiming Rites*, 10.

46. Vatican II, *Sacrosanctum concilium*, no. 10, in Flannery, 6.

7. Prayer and Decision-Making

1. See, for example, Sergio Bastianel, *Prayer in Christian Moral Life*, trans. Bernard Hoose (Middlegreen, England: St. Paul Publications, 1988).

2. For some practical suggestions for prayer and decision-making, see Jan Bots, "Praying in Two Directions: A Christian Method of Prayerful Decision-making," *Review for Religious* 41 (Jan.–Feb. 1982) : 58–64.

3. See, for example, James Gustafson, "Moral Discernment in the Christian Life," in *Norms and Context in Christian Ethics*, ed. Gene H. Outka and Paul Ramsey (New York: Charles Scribner's Sons, 1968), 17–36; and William C. Spohn, "The Reasoning Heart: An American Approach to Christian Discernment," *Theological Studies* 44 (March 1983) : 30–52.

4. Enda McDonagh, "The Meaning and Structure of Moral Experience," in *Gift and Call* (St. Meinrad, IN: Abbey Press, 1975), 17–39. See also McDonagh, "Morality and Prayer," in *Doing the Truth: The Quest for Moral Theology* (Notre Dame: University of Notre Dame, 1979), 40–57.

8. Decision-Making as Discernment

1. For a historical overview of Christian reflection on discernment, see Edward Malatesta et al., *Discernment of Spirits* (Collegeville, MN: Liturgical Press, 1970). This is a re-publication of the articles on discernment that appear in the *Dictionnaire de Spiritualité*, III, cols. 1222–1291.

2.   See, for example, the two scholarly and informative works of Jules Toner: *A Commentary on Saint Ignatius' Rules for the Discernment of Spirits: A Guide to the Principles and Practice* (St. Louis: Institute of Jesuit Studies, 1982); and *Discerning God's Will: Ignatius of Loyola's Teaching on Christian Decision Making* (St. Louis: Institute of Jesuit Sources, 1991). For a slightly more accessible discussion of the Ignatian view of discernment, see Piet Penning de Vries, *Discernment of Spirits: According to the Life and Teachings of St. Ignatius of Loyola*, trans. W. Dudok Van Heel (New York: Exposition Press, 1973). Any attempt to understand discernment fully requires attention to such studies of Ignatian thought. The present article, however, is not meant to build exclusively on the Ignatian reflections on discernment.

3.   See, for example, Thomas Dubay, *Authenticity: A Biblical Theology of Discernment* (Denville, NJ: Dimension Books, 1977); Thomas Green, *Weeds Among the Wheat* (Notre Dame: Ave Maria, 1984); Ernest Larkin, *Silent Presence: Discernment as Process and Problem* (Denville, NJ: Dimension Books, 1981); and David Lonsdale, *Listening to the Music of the Spirit: The Art of Discernment* (Notre Dame: Ave Maria, 1992).

4.   See, for example, William A. Barry, *Spiritual Direction and the Encounter with God: A Theological Inquiry* (New York: Paulist, 1992), 72–88; and Robert F. Morneau, *Spiritual Direction: Principles and Practices* (New York: Crossroad, 1992), 29–52.

5.   Green, 57.

6.   Jules Toner, *Commentary*, 12–15.

7.   Toner discusses conditions for and obstacles to authentic discernment at some length (*Discerning God's Will*, 70–101). Morneau summarizes ten principles of discernment (*Spiritual Direction*, 29–52).

8.   Philip Keane offers a summary analysis of a few of these reflections on moral discernment up to 1974 in his article

"Discernment of Spirits: A Theological Reflection," *American Ecclesiastical Review* 168 (1974): 43–61. Richard Gula offers a brief but valuable discussion of discernment at the end of his excellent introduction to Catholic moral theology, *Reason Informed by Faith: Foundations of Catholic Morality* (New York: Paulist, 1989), 314–29.

9.   Toner, *Discerning God's Will*, 30–33.

10. Gula notes a tension in pre–Vatican II Catholic moral theology in its understanding of the various levels of moral reflection. Following the tradition of St. Thomas, Catholic moral theology viewed the moral life itself teleologically—that is, as directed toward an "ultimate end" which is communion with God. It also generally derived rules or norms for action teleologically—that is, rules arise from the inherent tendencies of the human person to attain those goods that serve authentic human flourishing. But when it came to identifying one's concrete duty in particular situations, moral theology turned to deontology—that is, one's moral duty and correct choices were viewed as a following of the established rules and norms. The rule rather than the end or goal sought came to determine one's actual duty in concrete situations. See Gula, 301.

11. Enda McDonagh discusses the relationship between prayer and morality in pre-Vatican II moral theology in "Morality and Prayer," in *Doing the Truth: The Quest for Moral Theology* (Notre Dame: University of Notre Dame, 1979), 42–45.

12. See, for example, Romanus Cessario, *The Moral Virtues and Theological Ethics* (Notre Dame: University of Notre Dame Press, 1991); and Jean Porter, *The Recovery of Virtue: The Relevance of Aquinas for Christian Ethics* (Louisville, KY: Westminster/John Knox Press, 1990).

13. John Mahoney, "The Spirit and Moral Discernment in Aquinas," in *Seeking the Spirit: Essays in Moral and Pastoral Theology* (Denville, NY: Dimension Books, 1981), 63–80; René Simon, "The Moral Law and Discernment," in *Discernment of*

Spirits, Concilium 119, ed. Casiano Floristán and Christian Duqouc (New York: Crossroad/Seabury, 1979), 74–83. Mahoney has written several useful articles on discernment. In addition to the article cited above, three others are collected in the same book: "The Spirit and Community Discernment in Aquinas" (pp. 81–96), "'The Church of the Holy Spirit' in Aquinas" (pp. 97–117), and "Discernment of Spirits" (pp. 118–34). More recently, he has written "Conscience, Discernment, and Prophecy in Moral Decision Making," in *Riding Time Like a River: The Catholic Moral Tradition Since Vatican II*, ed. William J. O'Brien (Washington: Georgetown University, 1993), 81–97.

14. The classic modern study of prudence (and the other cardinal virtues) is offered by Josef Pieper, *Prudence*, trans. Richard and Clara Winston (New York: Pantheon, 1959). See also Daniel Mark Nelson, *The Priority of Prudence: Virtue and Natural Law in Thomas Aquinas and the Implications for Modern Ethics* (University Park, PA: Pennsylvania State University Press, 1992).

15. Bernard Häring, *The Law of Christ: Moral Theology for Priests and Laity* (Westminster: Cork, 1961), I:491.

16. Mahoney, "The Spirit and Moral Discernment," 67.

17. See, for example, Christopher Kiesling, "The Seven *Quiet* Gifts of the Holy Spirit," *The Living Light* 23 (Jan. 1987): 137–46; and Anthony J. Kelly, "The Gifts of the Holy Spirit: Aquinas and the Modern Context," *The Thomist* 38 (April 1974): 193–231. Kelly suggests a reinterpretation of Aquinas' teaching on the gifts in light of Lonergan's intentionality analysis.

18. Gula offers a helpful summary of these three models (pages 20–21; 300–306).

19. See Gula, 123–62.

20. Vatican II, *Gaudium et spes*, no. 12, in *Vatican II: The Conciliar*

and Post Conciliar Documents, ed. Austin Flannery (Collegeville: Liturgical, 1975), 913–14.

21. Pope John Paul II, in arguing against contemporary trends toward moral relativism and subjectivism, reaffirms the council's teaching on conscience but cautions that conscience must act in accord with an objective moral order. See his encyclical letter, *Veritatis splendor*, nos. 54–64 (Washington: USCC, 1993), 85–98.

22. See: Karl Rahner, "On the Question of a Formal Existential Ethics," in *Theological Investigations*, trans. Karl-H. Kruger (New York: Seabury, 1963), 217–34; and "The Logic of Concrete Individual Knowledge in Ignatius Loyola," in *The Dynamic Element in the Church, Quaestiones Disputatae* 12, trans. W.J. O'Hara (New York: Herder and Herder, 1964), 84–170. A helpful summary and analysis is offered by Jeremy Miller in "Rahner's Approach to Moral Decision Making," *Louvain Studies* 5 (Fall 1975): 350–59.

23. Rahner, "Formal Existential Ethics," 227–28.

24. Karl Rahner, *Nature and Grace; and Other Essays*, trans. Dinah Wharton (New York: Sheed and Ward, 1963), 62–63.

25. Philip S. Keane, *Christian Ethics and Imagination* (New York: Paulist, 1984).

26. Gula, 185–98. Gula draws much of his discussion from the work of Protestant ethicist James Gustafson: *Christ and the Moral Life* (Chicago: University of Chicago Press, 1968), 238–71. The emphasis on the centrality of the distinctive Christian character in the Christian moral life is especially associated with the work of Stanley Hauerwas. See, for example, Stanley Hauerwas, *Character and the Christian Life: A Study in Theological Ethics*, Trinity University Monograph Series in Religion 3 (San Antonio: Trinity University Press, 1975).

27. See: James Gustafson, "Moral Discernment in the Christian

Life," in *Norm and Context in Christian Ethics*, ed. Gene H. Outka and Paul Ramsey (New York: Charles Scribner's Sons, 1968), 17–36; and *Ethics from a Theocentric Perspective*, vol. 1: *Theology and Ethics* (Chicago: University of Chicago Press, 1981).

28. William C. Spohn, "The Reasoning Heart: An American Approach to Christian Discernment" *Theological Studies* 44 (March 1983): 30–52.

29. Spohn, 52.

30. Daniel C. Maguire, *The Moral Choice* (Minneapolis: Winston, 1978). Stephen Happel and James J. Walter build on Maguire's discussion of the elements of moral choice and place it in a more explicitly Christian context. See Happel and Walter, *Conversion and Discipleship: A Christian Foundation for Ethics and Doctrine* (Philadelphia: Fortress, 1986), 167–73.

31. Daniel C. Maguire and A. Nicholas Fargnoli, *On Moral Grounds: The Art/Science of Ethics* (New York: Crossroad, 1991).

32. Enda McDonagh comes to a similar judgment about the "foundational moral experience," arguing that it is the experience of the other person as a "gift" that embodies a "call." See "The Meaning and Structure of Moral Experience," in *Gift and Call: Towards a Christian Theology of Morality* (St. Meinrad, IN: Abbey Press, 1975), 17–39. McDonagh relates this foundational moral experience with Christian prayer in "Morality and Prayer," in *Doing the Truth*, 40–57.

33. Maguire and Fargnoli, 34.

34. Gula, in briefly discussing the process of moral decision-making, draws together Gustafson's reflections on moral discernment and Maguire's earlier reflections on the elements of moral choice (pp. 305–306). For other studies that suggest the importance of various broader elements in Christian moral decision-making, see Vincent E. Rush, *The Responsible Christian:*

A Popular Guide to Moral Decision Making According to Classical Tradition (Chicago: Loyola University Press, 1984). Rush offers a brief summary of these elements on pages 118–19 and 238 of his work. See also Kenneth Overberg, *Conscience in Conflict: How to Make Moral Choices* (Cincinnati: St. Anthony Messenger Press, 1991); and Charles Shelton, "Discernment in Everyday Life: Spiritual and Psychological Considerations," *Spirituality Today* 34 (Winter 1982): 326–34.

35. Spohn, 40.

36. For an Orthodox perspective on decision-making including the importance of deification as well as other important elements, see Stanley S. Harakas, *Toward Transfigured Life: The Theoria of Eastern Orthodox Ethics* (Minneapolis, MN: Light and Life, 1983), 212–28.

INDEX